STUDIES IN THE UK

UK unemployment

Andrew Clark and Richard Layard
The London School of Economics
and Political Science

HEINEMANN EDUCATIONAL

For F.L.C. and J.A.G.C.; J.W.L. and D.L.

Heinemann Educational,
a division of Heinemann Educational Books Ltd
Halley Court, Jordan Hill,
Oxford, OX2 8EJ

OXFORD LONDON EDINBURGH
MELBOURNE SYDNEY AUCKLAND
SINGAPORE MADRID IBADAN
NAIROBI GABORONE HARARE
KINGSTON PORTSMOUTH NH(USA)

© Andrew Clark and Richard Layard 1989

First published 1989
Reprinted 1990

> British Library Cataloguing in Publication Data
> Clark, Andrew
>   UK unemployment. – (Studies in the UK economy).
>   1. Great Britain. Unemployment
>   I. Title II. Layard, Richard III. Series
>   331.13'7941

ISBN 0 435 33008 X

Typeset and illustrated by Gecko Limited, Bicester, Oxon
Printed and bound in Great Britain by Biddles Ltd, Guildford and King's Lynn

Acknowledgements

We are very grateful to Bryan Hurl for his time and effort in suggesting innumerable improvements to the original typescript. Thanks are also due to Sue Kirkbridge for typing under pressure, and to Andy Sentance for help with the data.

Acknowledgements are also due to the following for permission to reproduce copyright material: *The Economist* for the article on pp. 68–70; *Financial Times* for the article on pp. 39–40 and the graphic on p. 61; Terry O'Shaughnessy for the article on pp. 60–62 which appeared in the *Financial Times*; *The Times* for the letter on p. 43 and the article on pp. 44–45; Andrew Veitch for the article on pp. 66–67 which appeared in *The Guardian*.

Preface

During the so-called 'golden age of Keynesianism' which lasted for 25 years after the Second World War, unemployment, it was universally agreed, had been slain, if not by a sword, then certainly by the pen of J.M. Keynes. However, the spiralling inflation and spiralling unemployment of the 1970s and 80s – caused by adverse shocks – themselves dealt a shock to standard macroeconomic theory as portrayed in conventional A-level texts.

The fastest-growing A-level subject of Economics reflects the growing awareness of the young seeking employability in a post-Keynesian world, so it is perhaps ironic that A-level and AS-level Economics texts do not seem to have caught up with the profession's heightened awareness of what has happened to the British economy.

As experts at the Centre for Labour Economics at the London School of Economics and Political Science, Andrew Clark and Richard Layard are well-placed to provide an easily read guide to give a comprehensive understanding of unemployment now that it is again firmly in the centre of current debate. Read in conjunction with the companion volume in this series, *Deindustrialization,* it provides essential, up-to-date theory and applied knowledge.

Bryan Hurl
Series Editor

Contents

Preface		*iii*
Chapter One	Some basic facts about unemployment	*1*
Chapter Two	The causes of unemployment	*21*
Chapter Three	The UK experience	*32*
Chapter Four	Myths about unemployment	*46*
Chapter Five	Remedies for unemployment	*52*
Chapter Six	The objections considered	*63*
Projects		*71*
Index		*73*

Chapter One
Some basic facts about unemployment

'*Everybody needs to be needed, and for many people a job is an essential element in feeling needed.*'   Charter for Jobs

Introduction
Unemployment in the United Kingdom is still very high by historical standards, especially in the North of England. It is the major social problem of our time. When there is so much work that needs doing and so many people wanting to do it, our society is clearly failing if it cannot bring the two together.

Yet many people doubt whether anything like full employment is possible ever again. As in the 1930s, they consider high unemployment an act of God – the product of forces beyond our power to control. However, after the 1930s came the 1950s and 60s when unemployment was lower than in any previous period. Our present high unemployment is quite abnormal: it could be much lower. So in this book we shall begin by setting out the basic facts. In later chapters we discuss how unemployment came to be as high as it is, at some myths about this rise, and at possible solutions.

Trends
Figure 1 shows UK unemployment rates since the last century. The many peaks and troughs indicate that this rate has changed often, and many times quite sharply, over the period indicated.

Certain of these peaks and troughs can be identified as relating to well-known events. High unemployment rates in the late nineteenth century and in the 1930s reflect the Great Depression of 1873-96 and the deeper Depression of the 1930s respectively. Very low unemployment rates were observed in the periods of the first and second World Wars. Low unemployment rates continued on from the 1940s into the 1950s and the early 1960s. This was the time of the UK's long-lived post-war economic boom.

Since 1966, however, unemployment in the UK has risen practically continuously. It fell only in 1973 and 1979. The two big rises in

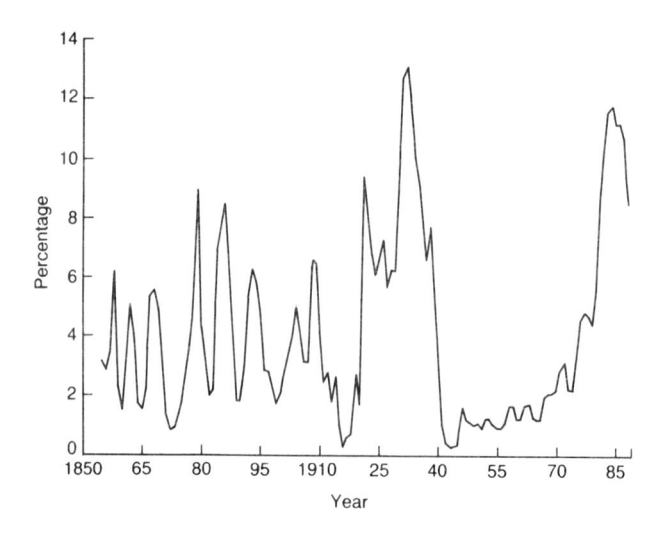

Figure 1 UK unemployment rates, 1855–1988

unemployment occurred between 1974 and 1976 and between 1980 and 1982 - after the first and second oil price **shocks** respectively. (In economic language a shock describes an unforeseen event which disturbs the economic system.) Unemployment fell from 1986 onwards.

Figure 2 shows the recent unemployment experience of the UK and US economies. The US experience is in sharp contrast to that of the UK: though unemployment has had an upward trend somewhat since the 1960s boom (associated with the Vietnam War), it is now little higher than in the 1950s. Moreover it fell sharply between 1982 and 1984, owing to expansionary government budgets, and has continued to fall up to the time of writing. The experience of the US in turning round a high and rising level of unemployment should remind us that recent domestic rises in unemployment are not permanent, nor are they induced by high technology.

Definitions

What do we mean by an 'unemployed person'? The definition used in Figures 1 and 2 is based on the UK's **Labour Force Survey**. This is a survey of the population in private households in the UK, carried out on behalf of the Department of Employment. It has been designed to gather information on a wide range of characteristics of the population which are related to employment and unemployment. According

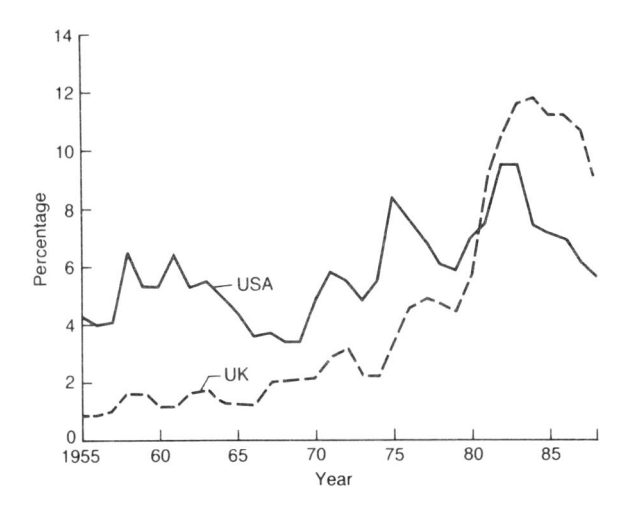

Figure 2 Unemployment rates for the UK and USA

to the survey people are counted as unemployed if they are seeking work but do not have it. They must also be in a position to start work.

This is a very natural definition of unemployment – a person has to be out of work *and* looking for work. The first part of this concept is very clear, because we can all see whether someone is not at work. However, the second concept is much more fuzzy, since there are many different levels of intensity with which people may seek work. The concept of 'seeking work' is especially unclear in relation to those married women who have not been working but now start to keep their eyes open in case a suitable job turns up. Thus the concept of male unemployment is more clearly defined than that of female unemployment. This is especially so for males aged 25 to 55 – nearly

Table 1 Unemployment rates by sex, April 1987

	Males	*Females*	*All*
UK	11.3	10.3	10.9
France	8.4	13.6	10.7
Germany	5.6	8.1	6.6
Italy	7.1	17.1	10.6
Sweden	1.9	1.9	1.9
Japan	2.7	2.8	2.8
US	5.9	6.2	6.1

all of these who are not employed are unemployed (apart from 3 per cent, most of whom are invalids or students). It is therefore interesting to look separately at male unemployment (see Table 1). In terms of this the UK performs much less favourably with other countries than in terms of overall unemployment.

The figures we have given so far are based on the standard definition of unemployment. This differs from the so-called **official unemployment figures** published each month in Britain, which are based on the numbers of job-seekers getting unemployment benefits (Unemployment Benefit or Income Support). These figures greatly under state female unemployment, for married women are not normally eligible for Income Support, nor for Unemployment Benefit if they opted out of making National Insurance contributions. Thus female unemployment in the UK, as measured by the official registered figures, does not correspond at all well to the standard definition of unemployment. For example, in the spring of 1986 the Labour Force Survey measure of unemployment for women was nearly 200 000 higher than the official unemployment figure. In addition, from 1988 onwards it has been made progressively more difficult to get unemployment benefits. Whether or not this is a good thing, it sometimes means that the trend in the official unemployment figures exaggerates the fall in unemployment as measured by the Labour Force Survey.

Figure 3 shows how the Department of Employment reconciled the Labour Force Survey definition of unemployment (the ILO/OECD definition) with the official unemployment figures or 'claimant count' of those getting benefits.

The difference of 200 000 in the two figures is made up of several large counter-balancing numbers. The claimant count includes 210 000 people who are employed and 860 000 people who are 'economically inactive', giving a total of 1 070 000 to be deducted. However there are 870 000 people who are unemployed on the Survey definition but who do not get benefits. Three-quarters of the non-claimant unemployed were women and about 70 per cent of these were married. This reinforces the point we made earlier about the accuracy of measures of female unemployment.

Counting the unemployed

A separate matter is how the official unemployed are counted. Frequent allegations of 'moving the goal posts' have been made by critics of the government whenever changes are brought in that reduce the government's estimate of unemployment.

Two issues of the Unemployment Unit's *Bulletin* (winter 1986 and

Some basic facts about unemployment

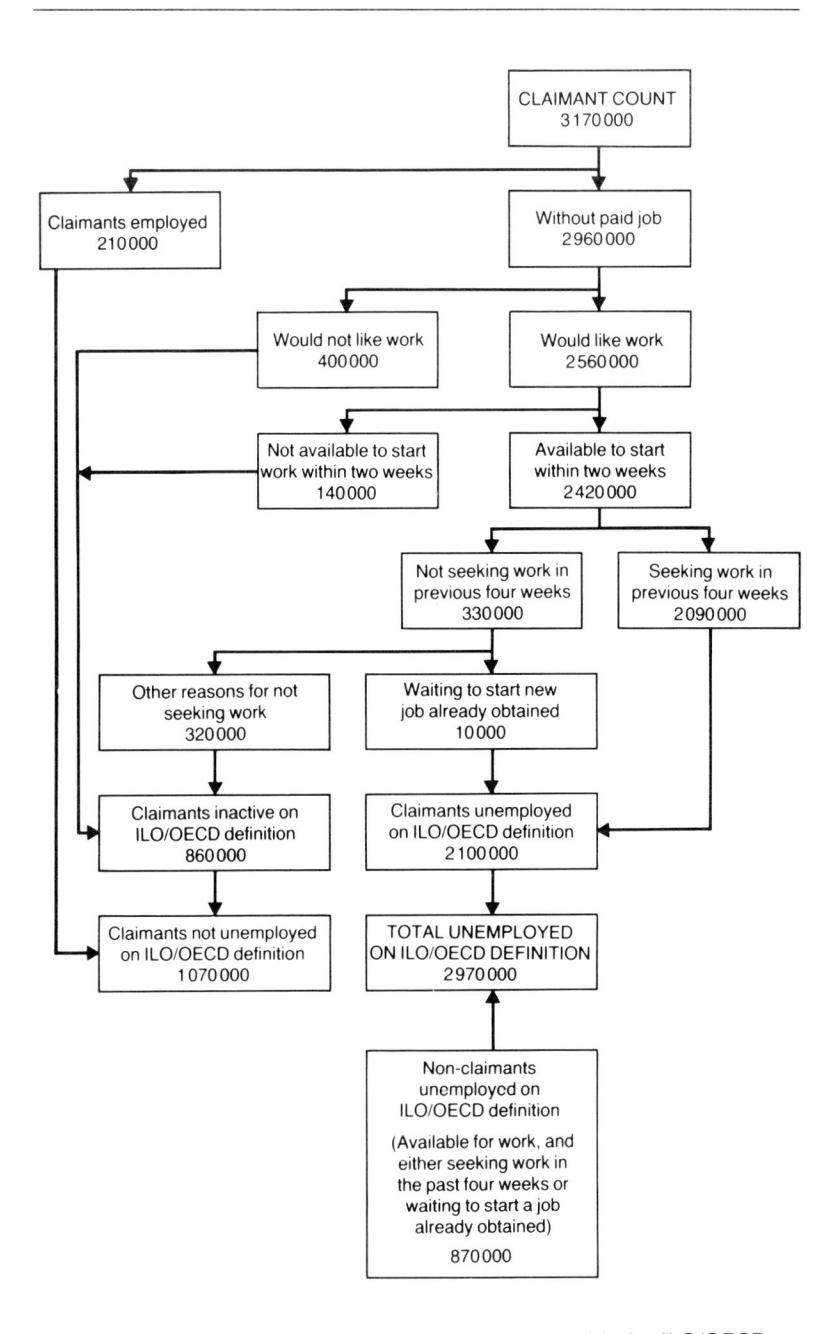

```
                            ┌──────────────────┐
                            │  CLAIMANT COUNT  │
                            │     3 170 000    │
                            └──────────────────┘
                    ┌──────────────┴──────────────┐
                    ▼                             ▼
         ┌────────────────────┐        ┌────────────────────┐
         │ Claimants employed │        │  Without paid job  │
         │      210 000       │        │     2 960 000      │
         └────────────────────┘        └────────────────────┘
                                   ┌──────────┴──────────┐
                                   ▼                     ▼
                       ┌────────────────────┐  ┌────────────────────┐
                       │ Would not like work│  │  Would like work   │
                       │      400 000       │  │     2 560 000      │
                       └────────────────────┘  └────────────────────┘
                                            ┌──────────┴──────────┐
                                            ▼                     ▼
                               ┌────────────────────┐  ┌────────────────────┐
                               │ Not available to start│ │ Available to start │
                               │ work within two weeks │ │  within two weeks  │
                               │      140 000         │  │     2 420 000      │
                               └────────────────────┘  └────────────────────┘
                                                    ┌──────────┴──────────┐
                                                    ▼                     ▼
                                        ┌────────────────────┐  ┌────────────────────┐
                                        │ Not seeking work in│  │ Seeking work in    │
                                        │ previous four weeks│  │ previous four weeks│
                                        │      330 000       │  │     2 090 000      │
                                        └────────────────────┘  └────────────────────┘
                                     ┌────────────┴────────────┐
                                     ▼                         ▼
                          ┌────────────────────┐  ┌────────────────────┐
                          │ Other reasons for not│ │ Waiting to start new│
                          │   seeking work      │  │ job already obtained│
                          │      320 000        │  │       10 000        │
                          └────────────────────┘  └────────────────────┘
                                     ▼                         ▼
                          ┌────────────────────┐  ┌────────────────────┐
                          │ Claimants inactive on│ │Claimants unemployed │
                          │  ILO/OECD definition │ │ on ILO/OECD definition│
                          │      860 000         │ │     2 100 000       │
                          └────────────────────┘  └────────────────────┘
                                     ▼                         ▼
                          ┌────────────────────┐  ┌────────────────────┐
                          │Claimants not unemployed│ │ TOTAL UNEMPLOYED  │
                          │ on ILO/OECD definition │ │ON ILO/OECD DEFINITION│
                          │     1 070 000          │ │    2 970 000      │
                          └────────────────────┘  └────────────────────┘
                                                            ▲
                                        ┌────────────────────┐
                                        │   Non-claimants    │
                                        │   unemployed on    │
                                        │ ILO/OECD definition│
                                        │                    │
                                        │(Available for work, and│
                                        │ either seeking work in │
                                        │ the past four weeks or │
                                        │ waiting to start a job │
                                        │   already obtained)    │
                                        │      870 000       │
                                        └────────────────────┘
```

Figure 3 The monthly claimant count compared with the ILO/OECD measure of unemployment in the UK, spring 1986

Summer 1988) listed 24 changes to the way in which the official unemployment total has been computed since 1979. Some of these changes have had a large effect. For example, the decision in October 1982 to count only benefit claimants – as opposed to those registered at Jobcentres or Careers Offices – as unemployed is estimated to have removed between 170 and 190 thousand people from the count. More recently the provisions of the Social Security Act 1988 which deny benefit to almost all 16- and 17-year-olds have reduced the figure by almost 100 thousand.

The Unemployment Unit calculates unemployment figures using the definition that was in force in 1979. The estimates of unemployment shown in Table 2 indicate the extent to which changes in the definition since then have altered the figures.

Table 2 UK unemployment, January 1989

	Unemployment Unit estimates (1979 definition)	Department of Employment figures (current definition)
Seasonally adjusted	2 678 900 (9.4%)	1 988 100 (7.0%)

Whether the changes to the count are a good thing or not is a separate issue. It is, however, important that comparisons of unemployment figures over time should use *consistent* definitions, otherwise differences due to counting technique could easily be allocated to changed labour market conditions.

By this stage you may be wondering whether the concept of unemployment means anything at all and whether we should be worried about it, since it seems to be difficult to measure. We feel emphatically that unemployment is important and that we should certainly worry about it. First, unemployment represents **economic inefficiency**. If in one year 10 per cent of the workforce is unemployed, then output will be about 10 per cent lower than it could have been (depending upon who the unemployed are). This represents a waste of our national resources. Second, on **equity** grounds, unemployment reflects human suffering in terms of low income and low self-esteem.

Consider, first, income. In the 1930s the income levels on the 'dole' were much lower than today both in real terms and relative to income in work, so that it can be argued that suffering was greater then. Between countries, the incomes of the unemployed (relative to the employed) are lower in the US than in Britain, but lower in Britain than in the rest of northern Europe.

As regards self-esteem, the effect of unemployment depends a great deal on how long a person has been unemployed. There is much evidence that people's morale sinks progressively as their unemployment lengthens. A person who has been unemployed for two years suffers far more each week than does one who has been unemployed for two weeks. So it is very important to know how long people have been unemployed.

How long does it last?

The answer in the UK is 'Depressingly long'. Currently, nearly half of all unemployed men have now been unemployed for over a year, and the 'average' unemployed man has been unemployed for a year and three-quarters.

Even more striking, most of the increase in unemployment has been via those who are experiencing **long-term unemployment** (out of work for over a year). This is shown in Figure 4. The number of long-term unemployed men rose from 100 000 in 1974 to about a million in 1986, although it has since fallen.

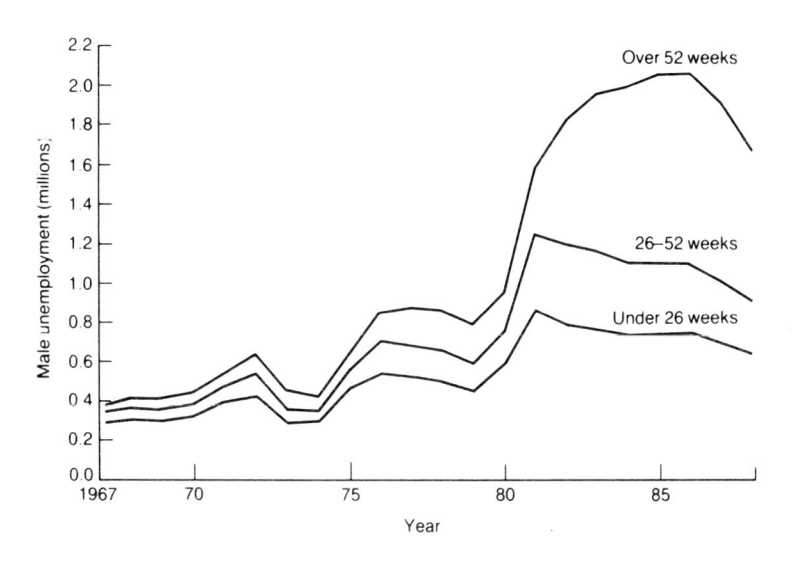

Figure 4 Male unemployment by duration, 1967–88 (these figures are from the official count)

There is an important lesson in this rise in long-term unemployment. The number of people who become unemployed each year has risen relatively little. For example, the number of unemployed with less than two weeks' unemployment experience was the same in 1975 as in 1985, though total unemployment was up nearly three-fold. So if there has been no change in the number of people becoming unemployed, then why did unemployment rise so dramatically in the 1980s? The answer is that the people who are becoming unemployed are staying unemployed for much longer. The majority of people now, as earlier, are never unemployed, while those who do become unemployed now suffer far more than they used to.

To help us understand what is happening, let us apply a simple rule of thumb. This says that, when unemployment is constant, the number of people who are unemployed at any time equals the number who become unemployed each week *times* the average number of weeks they remain unemployed.

Unemployed = entrants per week × weeks unemployed.

By analogy, the number of school students *equals* the number of first-year students *times* the length of the course. In the 'school of unemployment' the number of students has risen mainly not because of new entrants but because of a depressing increase in the length of the course.

Our formula makes it clear that 10 per cent unemployment could reflect two extreme cases (or anything in between):

- everyone becomes unemployed once a year, for on average 10 per cent of the year; or
- ten per cent become unemployed each year, for on average a year.

It happens that the latter is far closer to the UK situation than the former.

As we shall see later on, this fact provides an important clue about how to reduce unemployment: we should concentrate on reducing long-term unemployment, and avoid trying to reduce the proportion of people who become unemployed. For this latter proportion is a powerful force restraining **wage inflation** (defined as the change in money wage levels over time), while long-term unemployment is not and therefore represents a total waste.

Given that long-term unemployment seems to be an important piece of the jigsaw, it is reasonable to ask why it is that it rose by such a large proportion when total unemployment rose. Might this even give us some ideas as to why unemployment has stayed high in the first place? Some suggestive evidence comes from comparing the durations of unemployment in different countries and relating this to their **social security systems** – that is the rules defining who can get what kinds of benefits and for how long. As Figure 5 shows, unemployment is very much shorter in Sweden and the USA than in the main European countries. Why is this? An obvious factor is the social security system. In the USA, Unemployment Insurance runs out after six months. After that the unemployed can in some states get a much reduced income on 'social assistance', but in many states (including 'enlightened' Massachusetts) a childless man who has been out of work for over six months gets nothing. In Sweden benefit lasts a maximum of 300 days. By then the person will normally have been offered a place on a training or work programme – and if he refuses that, he ceases to be eligible for benefit. By contrast, in Germany benefits continue indefinitely (though at a reduced rate after a year). In France they continue for nearly four years. In Britain, for somebody already on Supplementary Benefit there is no reduction in income whatever as time goes on.

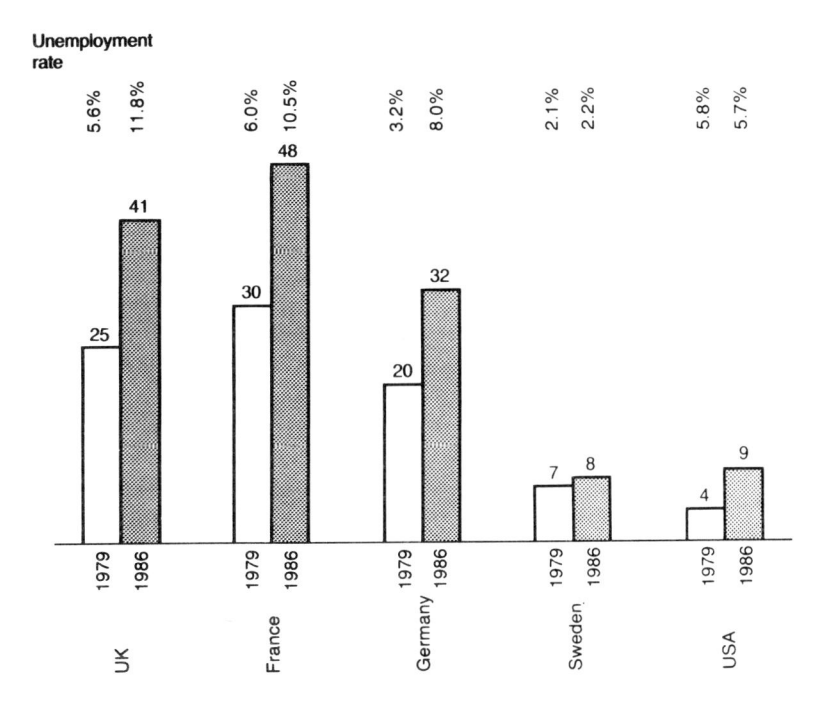

Figure 5 Percentage of unemployed adults out of work for over a year

It is noticeable that countries which have open-ended social security not only have high long-term unemployment but have also experienced the largest rises in unemployment. This raises the question as to whether, when countries are subjected to a shock which depresses output and employment (such as the second oil price rise), they are more likely to develop a culture of unemployment if they have open-ended benefits. Such a benefit system may reduce incentives for the long-term unemployed to seek work, and may thus make it more difficult to reduce unemployment in Europe, unless specific measures are developed to deal with the problem of the long-term unemployed.

How do people become unemployed?

In the discussion so far we have avoided any classification of the unemployed as *voluntary* or *involuntary*. Unemployment is, of course, affected by individual choices but by much else besides. However, it is reasonable to ask how individuals actually come to be unemployed.

The majority of unemployed men have either lost their job through **redundancy**, left their last job three or more years ago, or have never had a job. The proportion of unemployed men who had been dismissed rose markedly from 1979 to 1981 but has since fallen back to its earlier level. In addition, the proportion of unemployed men who had never worked before has been stable at about 10 per cent in each year. Among married women the proportion who were dismissed in the past three years or who had never had a full-time job is much smaller. More of them left their last job three or more years ago, and it is likely that many of these are married women trying to get back to work after child-rearing. The detailed picture is in Table 3.

Which occupations and age-groups are most affected?

It is time now to ask who the unemployed actually are: What are their skills? How old are they? Where do they live and in which industries did they used to work? The answer is that the typical unemployed person is low-skilled, young, from the northern half of the UK, and with a background in manufacturing or construction.

Skills

Let us start with the **skill mix**. In Britain in 1985, 84 per cent of unemployed men were manual workers, half of them semi- or unskilled. The corresponding unemployment rates were:

Non-manual	4 per cent
Skilled manual	11 per cent
Semi- and unskilled	22 per cent

Table 3 How people came to be unemployed in the UK*

	Men	Married women	Single women	All
Seeking first job	11	4	26	12
Left last job 3 or more years ago	26	33	21	27
Left job within 3 years, of which main reason for leaving was:				
Made redundant from regular job	25	10	15	20
Temporary job ended	15	8	13	13
Resigned from regular job	6	7	8	7
Family, personal or health reasons	6	29	9	12
Other	10	6	7	9
	100	100	100	100

* The figures are rounded percentages from the spring of 1986.

There is nothing new about these differentials, which incidentally reflect differences in the number of people becoming unemployed rather than how long they have been unemployed. In fact the ratio between the different unemployment rates has varied little over time. Ten or fifteen years ago, as now, semi- and unskilled workers were roughly four times as likely to be unemployed as non-manual workers.

Age and unemployment

Another trait associated with different unemployment rates is **age**, as shown in Table 4. Unemployment rates are typically much higher for young people than for older people. Their higher unemployment rate arises entirely because they are more likely to become unemployed; but once unemployed they will remain so for a shorter period than older people.

High youth unemployment is due partly to the general economic situation and partly to the level of youth wages. Since the labour

Table 4 Male unemployment rates by age, January

	Under 18	18–19	20–24	25–54	55–59	Totals
1976	12	11	10	4	5	7
1980	10	11	9	6	6	7
1985	22	29	23	14	19	17
1988	13	20	15	11	16	12

Note that these percentage rates are not comparable over time, but do indicate the relative position of youth unemployment compared with other age groups.

market went sour in the 1970s, job prospects have probably declined more for young people than for others, as firms have cut back on hiring. But since 1979 everyone aged 16 has been guaranteed a one-year place on what was the Youth Opportunities Programme and is now the **Youth Training Scheme**, whereby school-leavers are put in training positions with work experience aimed at training them for a permanent job on completion of the placement. Entitlement to this scheme was extended to all 16-18 year olds, and since the autumn of 1988 all unemployed people of this age are required to accept a YTS position or lose their benefit entitlement. As a result unemployment rates rose no faster from 1980 to 1985 for the young than for the middle-aged. From 1985 to 1988 the effect of the youth scheme has been to cut unemployment rates for the young by more than the corresponding drop for the older age-groups.

The advent of compulsion for the under-18s to join the YTS or lose their benefit (and so not appear on the official registered unemployment count) means that the unemployment rate of under 18s will be zero in future. It will be interesting to see whether this scheme results in lower unemployment rates for 18-19 and 20-24 year olds in future, as under-18s are found permanent jobs via the YTS; or whether the YTS positions prove only temporary, and unemployment rates for groups other than the under-18s remain high.

As regards pay, in Germany, where youth pay is relatively lower than in Britain, the youth unemployment rate is about the same as the adult unemployment rate. But in Britain there is evidence that between 1965 and 1975 increases in relative youth pay pushed up relative youth unemployment. Since 1977 the relative pay of youths has not risen and the rise in youth unemployment reflects the general economic situation.

As we have said, the typical unemployed worker is young. He

certainly does not correspond to the common image of the unemployed married man with a large family claiming lots of benefit. In fact only 50 per cent of unemployed men are married, and only 19 per cent of them have two or more children. Thus most of them cannot possible be (unkindly) described as social security scroungers with large families.

Industries and regions

We must now take a look at the industrial and regional aspects of unemployment, which are closely related. We can begin by examining the changing pattern of employees in employment (see Figure 6).

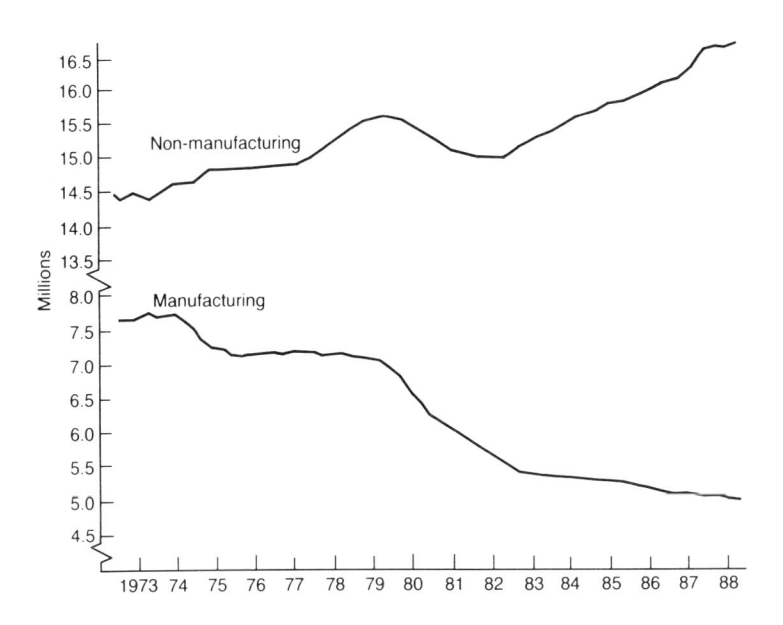

Figure 6 Manufacturing and non-manufacturing employees in employment in the UK

Since 1979 there has been an astounding collapse of manufacturing employment in Britain of over two million jobs – a much greater proportion than in any other major country. At the same time service employment has risen by much less than two million (falling until 1982 and then rising). This change in the structure of employment largely represents the **deindustrialization** that mature economies experience where concentration switches from industry towards services. So total employees in employment fell by over one million from June

1979 to June 1988, though this was offset by a roughly equal rise in self-employment. Given the masculinity of manufacturing it is not surprising that male employment has fallen, while female employment has improved over the period.

The fall in manufacturing employment has hurt some areas more than others, especially the West Midlands and the North of England. Thus unemployment has risen more (in terms of percentage points) in the areas which already had high unemployment.

In Figure 7 we can see some of the differences in unemployment rates between different regions. Unemployment is not evenly spread across the country. These figures, of course, conceal immense variations within regions, where some towns have become industrial deserts. There are still whole streets in the North of England (let alone Northern Ireland) where most people are out of work. But, taking quite large travel-to-work areas and using the official registered unemployment figures, here are some horror stories: Londonderry 26 per cent, Lanarkshire 16 per cent, South Tyneside 20 per cent, Liverpool 17 per cent, Doncaster 16 per cent. By contrast the South of England can offer Crawley, Cambridge and Basingstoke, all at under 3 per cent.

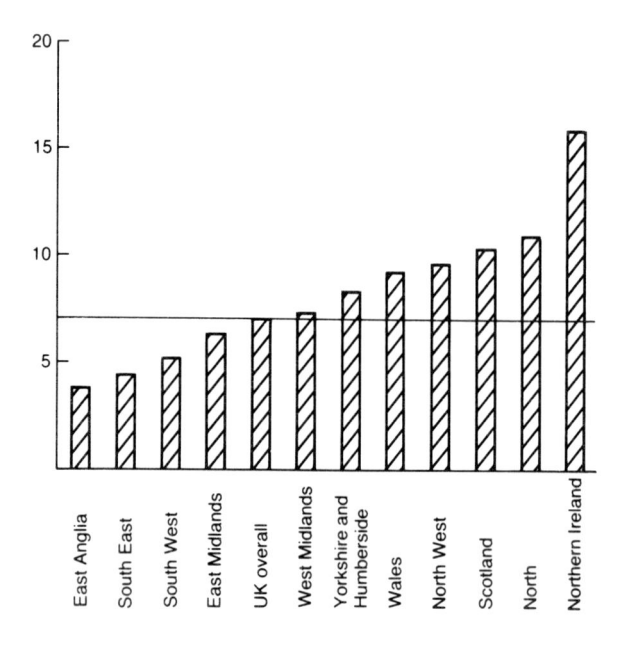

Figure 7 Unemployment rates by region, Jan. 1989

The industrial structure of unemployment (as opposed to employment) is not that clear a concept, since only 33 per cent of unemployed workers go back to the industry which they were in. But if we classify the unemployed by the last job they had then the situation in the early 1980s was as shown in Figure 8.

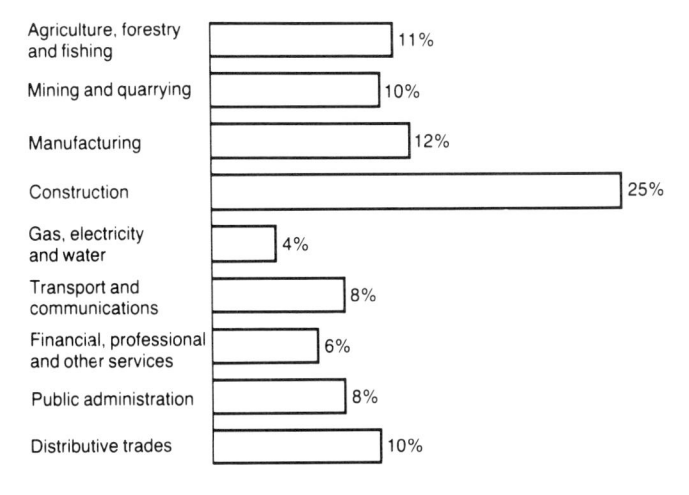

Industry	Unemployment rate
Agriculture, forestry and fishing	11%
Mining and quarrying	10%
Manufacturing	12%
Construction	25%
Gas, electricity and water	4%
Transport and communications	8%
Financial, professional and other services	6%
Public administration	8%
Distributive trades	10%

Figure 8 Unemployment rates by industry, May 1982

Clearly, some industries are always more unemployment-prone than others owing to the nature of the work that they offer. One obvious case from Figure 8 is construction, where building projects are often short-lived and workers are unemployed for a while in between projects. (This is another case where the differences in unemployment rates are mainly explained by differences in entry rates rather than duration.) Even so, the fall in employment in the 1980s hit manufacturing and construction very hard, and manufacturing and construction are still the industries with the highest unemployment rates.

Unemployment and vacancies

Like any other market, the labour market has buyers and sellers. Up to now we have concentrated on the sellers – the employed and the unemployed – but we shall now look at the behaviour of the demanders of labour too. In the same way that the unemployed can be regarded as frustrated retailers of labour, then firms with **vacancies** can be seen as frustrated purchasers of labour.

Vacancies are advertised in a wide number of ways: at Jobcentres, by private employment agencies, in newspapers, on vacancy boards, by word of mouth, and so on. It is then rather difficult to be precise about exactly how many vacancies exist at any one time.

For early 1988 we do have precise figures for the number of vacancies in the economy as a result of a survey undertaken at the request of the Department of Employment. This survey found that in a typical month there were a little over 700 000 vacancies in Great Britain.

For other time periods we have reliable information about the number of vacancies that are advertised at Jobcentres, and we can use this to estimate a figure for total vacancies.

Figure 9 shows the behaviour of unemployment and vacancies since 1956 by plotting one against the other in a 'U/V curve'. Both unemployment and vacancies are expressed as rates: unemployment is divided by the labour force (the sum of the people in work and the unemployed), while vacancies are divided by employees in employment. The 1950s and 60s were associated with low levels of unemployment and high vacancy rates, reflecting the tight labour market that existed in this period. The two oil shocks of 1973 and 1979 both pushed the curve in a south-easterly direction where there are fewer vacancies and more unemployment. Recent years have seen something of a recovery from unemployment, but the ratio of unemployment to vacancies is still very high compared with those that prevailed before 1973.

Figure 9 UK unemployment and vacancies

Despite the low ratio, 700 000 empty posts seem like a lot when there are over two million unemployed. The figures for London are 140 000 vacancies and 250 000 unemployed (on the claimant count). The existence of frustrated supply and demand together suggests that there is a degree of **mismatch** between the vacant jobs and the unemployed.

For example, suppose that workers could be split into just two types, the skilled and unskilled. Assume there are 200 people unemployed and 100 vacancies. Then it is possible to describe two cases, as illustrated in Figure 10. In the top panel there is perfect match, with the ratio of skilled to unskilled being exactly the same for both unemployment and vacancies. In the bottom panel, however, there is imperfect match, or mismatch, in that skilled workers account for only 20 per cent of the unemployed but 80 per cent of the vacancies.

Mismatch can occur for reasons other than skill. It is often said that the discrepancies between regional unemployment rates indicate mismatch, and that the situation is made worse by the difficulty of finding housing in the better-off regions. Mismatch may also result from a switch of demand from one industry to another – unemployment would then result in the declining sectors until workers could redeploy themselves into the sectors that are now expanding. This type of mismatch is obviously similar to structural unemployment.

PERFECT MATCH

	Skilled	Unskilled	Totals
Unemployed	40	160	200
Vacancies	20	80	100

IMPERFECT MATCH

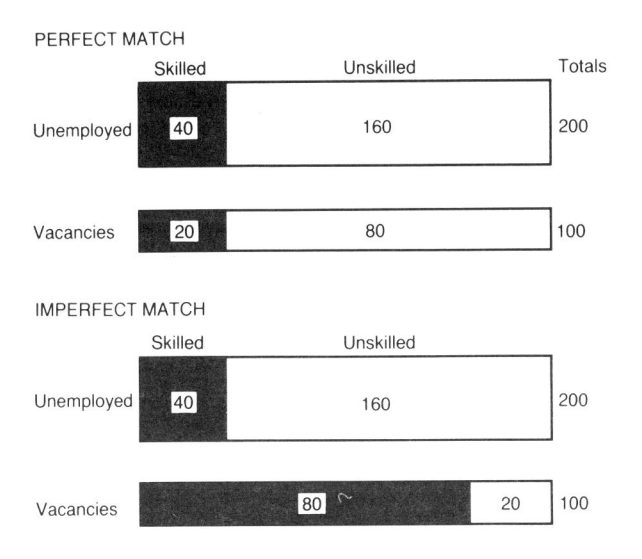

	Skilled	Unskilled	Totals
Unemployed	40	160	200
Vacancies	80	20	100

Figure 10 Mismatch (see the text)

The labour force and unemployment

Finally, there is an obvious question. Can the level of unemployment be explained by the size of the **labour force**? As a matter of arithmetic we know that

$$\text{Unemployment} = \text{labour force} - \text{employment}.$$

So if the labour force was lower and employment the same, unemployment would be reduced. In a later chapter we shall argue that over a longish run unemployment is not going to be affected by the labour force, since if the labour force rises, employment will rise. That has certainly been the case for most of the past two hundred years. But at this stage let us just look at the facts.

In the UK the labour force grew substantially from 1950 to 1966 (see Figure 11) and unemployment was pretty well stable. The labour force then fell for the next five years before resuming its previous growth rate (except between 1980 and 1983). For all of this period since 1966 (of both falling *and* rising labour force), unemployment rose.

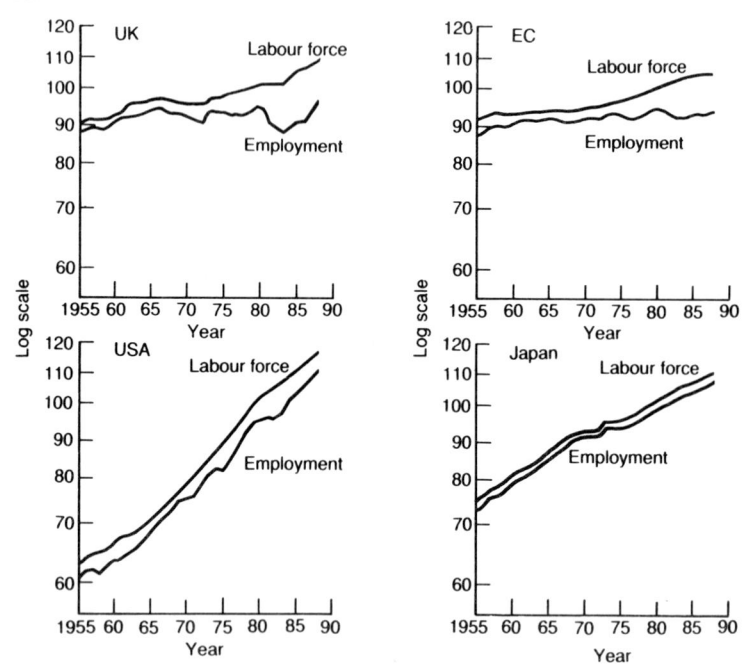

Figure 11 Labour force, employment and unemployment (the scale is indexed to 1979 labour force = 100)

The contrast with the USA and Japan is striking. In both of these countries the labour force rose much more than in the UK (or Europe); yet unemployment rose much less. We can easily see this by comparing the slopes of the lines in Figure 11.

So why did unemployment rise so much here? In the next chapter it will be time to make a systematic attempt to find out.

KEY WORDS

Shocks	Social security systems
Labour Force Survey	Redundancy
Official unemployment figures	Skill mix
	Age
Economic inefficiency	Youth Training Scheme
Equity	Deindustrialization
Long-term unemployment	Vacancies
	Mismatch
Wage inflation	Labour Force

Reading list

Armstrong, H. and Taylor, J., *Regional Policy: The Way Forward*, Employment Institute, 1987.

Armstrong, H. and Taylor, J., *Regional Economics*, Heinemann, in press.

Bazen, S., and Thirlwall, A.P., Chapter 4 in *Deindustrialization*, Heinemann Educational, 1989.

Johnson, C., Chapter 4 in *Measuring the Economy*, Penguin, 1988.

Southworth, M., 'Counting the jobless 1979-1986', *Economics*, 1987, vol. 23, p.1.

Treble, J., 'Unemployment: facts and theories', *Economic Review*, 1988, vol.6, no.2.

Essay topics

1. What kind of people are likely to be unemployed and why?
2. (a) Explain the relation between the duration of unemployment and the level of unemployment. (b) Does the duration of unemployment as such matter (for any given level of unemployment)?
3. 'The existence of thousands of vacancies while there are many out of work proves that the unemployed are work-shy.' Do you agree?

Data Response Question 1
Looking at unemployment trends

From your local library or an HMSO agent (see Yellow Pages) obtain a copy of a recent *Employment Gazette*, produced by the Department of Employment.

1. From Table 2.1 therein write down a series of the (official registered) seasonally adjusted UK unemployment rate as a percentage of the workforce for the past three or four years. Plot this series against time. What has happened over the past few years? Can you explain why?
2. From Table 2.3 of the *Gazette* obtain a corresponding series for your own regional unemployment rate. Draw this on the same graph that you used for question 1. Is your region higher or lower than the UK as a whole? Using this chapter, can you put forward any reasons why this difference exists?
3. From Table 2.4 of the *Gazette* obtain the current unemployment rate for your local travel-to-work area. Is it higher or lower than the figure given for the UK on the same page? (Note that these unemployment rates are defined slightly differently from those used in questions 1 and 2.) Try to find some areas of very high and very low unemployment. Is there evidence of a North-South divide? Are there some areas which do not fit into those simple categories? Can you explain why?

Chapter Two
The causes of unemployment

'If the Treasury were to fill old bottles with bank notes, bury them at suitable depths in disused coal-mines, which are then filled up to the surface with town rubbish, and leave it to private enterprise to dig the notes up again, there need be no more unemployment.' J. M. Keynes

What has gone wrong? Governments do not like unemployment and it is not good for their re-election prospects. So why do they not reduce it? The answer of course is that they also dislike **inflation**, and so do their electorates.

The only reason we have unemployment is that governments are using it to contain inflation. Generally, governments will not admit this. But if you suggest doing more to expand the economy, their answer will always be, 'That's inflationary'. In fact why else would they not do something desirable like creating jobs? clearly, they *are* using unemployment to control inflation.

Thus, to understand unemployment, we need to understand the relationship between unemployment and inflation, and what affects it.

Inflation and unemployment

If unemployment is low, inflation will tend to rise. Employers will find it more difficult to fill their vacancies. So they will try to attract workers by paying more than the going rate. At the same time unions will feel in a stronger position to push for wage increases. But, if unemployment is high enough, inflation will be stable; and, if it is even higher, inflation will actually fall, as happened in the early 1980s.

Thus there is a critical level of unemployment at which inflation will be just stable – neither rising nor falling. We shall call this the NAIRU (the **non-accelerating inflation rate of unemployment**) – a terrible phrase but one that has somehow become established. This is charted in Figure 12. If unemployment is pushed below the NAIRU, inflation increases; and if unemployment is pushed above this point, inflation can be reduced. The relationship between the change in inflation and the level of unemployment is shown by the sloping line. In the example chosen, the NAIRU is 10 per cent unemployment (or 2.8 million),

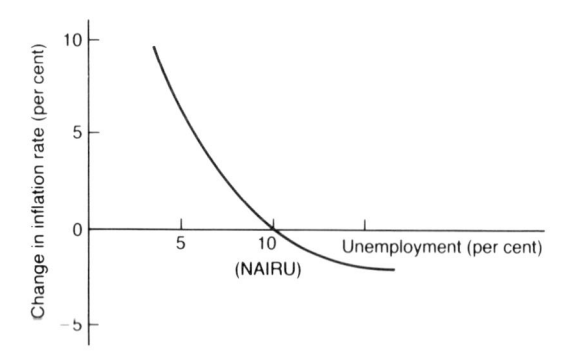

Figure 12 Unemployment and inflation (how inflation will rise if unemployment is below the NAIRU, and vice versa)

which may not be too far from the mark. Starting from the NAIRU, a 1 per cent lower level of unemployment would make inflation rise by about 1 per cent a year – again a reasonably plausible estimate.

One might ask why low unemployment leads to rising inflation, rather than simply to rising prices. In other words why, when unemployment is low, do we find *inflation* rising, rather than *prices* rising at a steady rate of inflation? The answer is that inflation has a momentum (or inertia) of its own. If there is no particular pressure in the labour market, people expect inflation to continue at its former level. So if prices are already rising they will continue to rise. Extra pressure in the labour market will make them rise faster. Economic agents then apply **adaptive expectations** to their decision-making; trade unions, for example, recalibrate upwards their wage demands expecting the higher level of inflation to continue.

To see how reasonable this whole argument is, Figure 13 shows the history of inflation relative to unemployment. The top panel shows the inflation rate. The next panel shows the unemployment rate adjusted for the estimated change in the NAIRU. It is shown on an inverted scale, so that peaks on the graph reflect peaks in economic activity. It is these peaks which cause inflation to increase, while troughs cause it to decrease.

Thus the final panel (c) plots together the unemployment peaks and troughs *and* the changes in inflation. This last graph provides a potted history of the last 30 years. As can be seen, inflation tended to rise in the booms of 1956, 1961, 1965 and 1970 (all of them related to elections!). In the slacker intervening periods, inflation tended to fall (or rise less). The boom of 1973, however, had an altogether disproportionate effect on inflation. This was because it coincided

The causes of unemployment

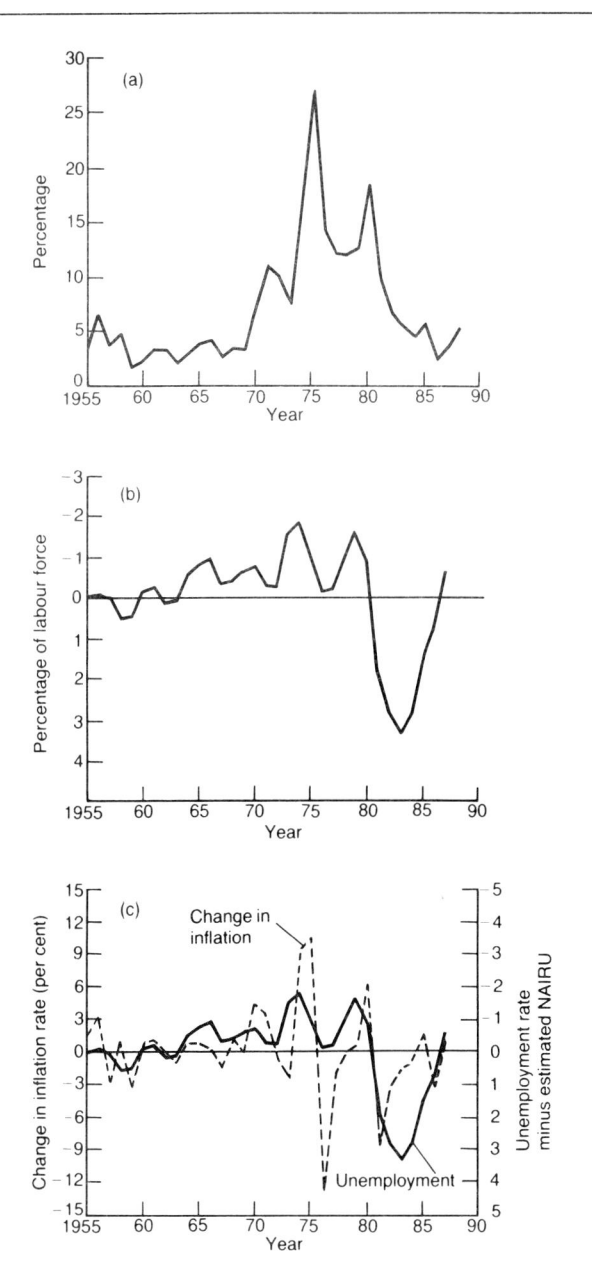

Figure 13 (a) shows inflation (the annual change in the GDP deflator). (b) shows unemployment (deviations from the estimated NAIRU). (c) shows unemployment and changes in inflation (the fall in inflation in 1976 was due mainly to incomes policy)

23

with booms in most other countries, leading to an explosion of **commodity prices** (such as copper, cotton, rice, wheat and zinc) and the accompanying first oil price rise. Matters were made much worse by the **indexation** arrangements, whereby wages were increased in accordance with movements in the Retail Price Index, as prescribed by the prevailing incomes policy. The passive policies of the incoming Labour government did nothing to dampen the fires of inflation, and by 1976 the situation was so critical that a drastic incomes policy (£6 a week for all, or 10 per cent for the average person) was introduced. This had a sensational effect in reducing inflation from 27 per cent in 1975 to 14 per cent the following year. The next inflationary surge came in 1979–80, following on the partial economic recovery of 1978–79 and the abandonment of the incomes policy. However this time the fire was put out by a huge dose of unemployment. This brought inflation down rapidly in 1981, and inflation since then has remained fairly much under control. It has not, however, continued to fall as much as one might have expected, and we discuss the reasons for this later in this chapter, when we consider the recent experience of the UK.

Thus there *is* a clear relationship between unemployment and inflation, but only if we recognize the fact that the NAIRU has risen.

We can summarize the lessons so far in terms of Figure 14. If unemployment is at the NAIRU, inflation is stable; but if more people are employed, inflation will tend to rise. The curve is the modern version of the so-called **Phillips curve**. The NAIRU is sometimes called the 'natural' rate of unemployment, but this is misleading because it seems to imply that it is inevitable. In fact, however, a major objective of policy is to reduce it.

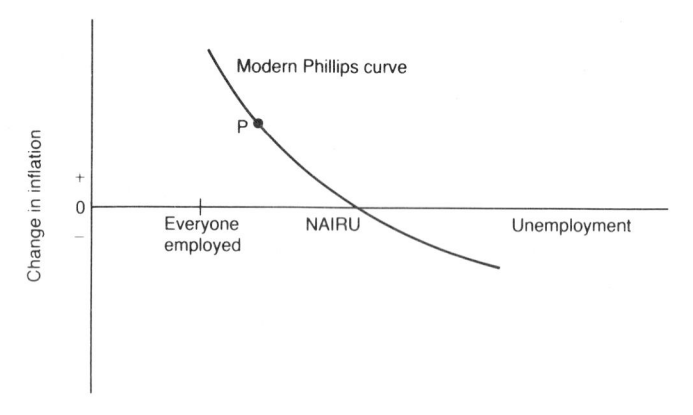

Figure 14 Application of the modern Phillips curve

In the long run (when inflation *has* to be stable) unemployment will settle down at the NAIRU. But in the short-term unemployment depends on the growth of aggregate money spending (or aggregate demand) relative to the inflation rate. Thus suppose that in the figure we were at the NAIRU last year and inflation was 5 per cent. This year money spending rose by 10 per cent. The result, as illustrated at point P in the figure, is a rise in inflation *and* a rise in employment. The split between extra inflation and extra employment depends on the slope of the Phillips curve (and on productivity growth). But a rise in the growth rate of money spending will *always* increase inflation and employment, compared with what they would otherwise be. The reverse is also true.

Thus, in the short term, employment and inflation are jointly determined by aggregate *money* demand and the aggregate supply behaviour summarized in the Phillips curve. The resulting level of output is generally called **real aggregate demand.**

The rise in unemployment

We can now come back to unemployment, and think of its rise as consisting of two parts:

- First, there is the rise in the NAIRU, which needs to be explained in detail.
- Second, there is an 'overkill' – a rise in unemployment above the NAIRU, resulting in a fall in inflation; or there is an 'underkill' – a fall in unemployment below the NAIRU, resulting in a rise in inflation.

The overkill or underkill

Let us start with the overkill, sometimes called Keynesian unemployment. In the short run the level of unemployment is determined by 'real aggregate demand', that is, by the demand for British output. In the early 1980s this demand fell sharply relative to our potential output, much of this fall resulting from government policy. The fall in demand raised unemployment by at least five percentage points. High priority was given to *reducing* inflation by reducing demand. From our discussion of Figure 12 it is obvious that a policy of reducing inflation will involve a rate of unemployment higher than the NAIRU – the overkill.

In a position where inflation is falling, there are two ways to ameliorate the unemployment position. The quickest is to raise employment by spending more money now, and accept that when the

NAIRU is reached inflation will still be at the present level. The alternative is not to boost money spending, but to rely on falling inflation to increase the real value of this spending. This takes much longer, but it also works. It is even possible that eventually, as in 1988, there may be a danger of underkill as real spending recovers. At this point, there will be signs of upwards pressure on inflation – or, in the language of science, of **overheating** – as the growth in demand outstrips the ability of the economy to supply goods without a rise in prices.

Factors affecting the NAIRU

So much for the 'demand-side' factors affecting unemployment. But there is also the rise in the NAIRU, which has reduced the ability of the economy to supply extra output without this leading to extra inflation. This is what people mean when they talk about the importance of improving the **supply side** of the economy. By this term they do not simply mean improving the supply of labour; they mean everything which affects the ability of the economy to provide a sustained supply of output at stable inflation.

So what factors may have increased the NAIRU? There are a whole host of possible explanations, including:

- the two oil price rises of 1973 and 1979
- the slowdown in productivity growth
- the rise in taxation
- easier access to social security benefits
- more mismatch between jobs available and the qualities of the unemployed
- employment protection (making it harder to sack workers once hired)
- increases in union militancy
- the likelihood that high unemployment in the recent past can raise the NAIRU, at least temporarily (this would help to explain why wage inflation is not now falling as much as one might expect).

All or any of these factors could have played a role, and we shall discuss some of the more salient ones in the next chapter. But, before we can do this, we need some general idea about how the NAIRU is determined. We can then use this framework to look at the factors which must affect it.

How the NAIRU is determined

The theory is very simple. In a nutshell, there is at any particular time a limit to the living standards which the economy can provide to its workers. In other words there is a **'feasible' real wage** (the money wage divided by the price index). If workers try to get more than this, inflation will increase – with wages accelerating and prices following them upwards. So stable inflation requires realistic behaviour at the bargaining table.

What ensures this? The answer is that there must be enough unemployment. Just enough unemployment will ensure that the **'target' real wage** demanded by the workers exactly equals the 'feasible' real wage. If there is 'not enough' unemployment, wages will be pushed too high and wage inflation will increase. Alternatively, if there is 'excess' unemployment, wage and price inflation will fall.

To make the matter more concrete, we have to look first at how firms set prices, and then at how wage-bargainers (both firms and unions) set wages. In the long run, the pricing behaviour of firms determines the real wage. For, whatever **money wage** is set, firms will set prices so as to bring the purchasing power of wages down to the normal level. Thus, suppose there is a normal **price mark-up** (of prices over wages), so that

Prices = wages × normal price mark-up.

It follows that the feasible real wage is given by

$$\text{Feasible real wage} = \frac{\text{wages}}{\text{prices}} = \frac{1}{\text{normal price mark-up}}$$

This is shown as a horizontal line in Figure 15. Clearly the feasible real wage will be affected by the degree of **monopoly** in product markets and many other variables discussed below. It is not a technological

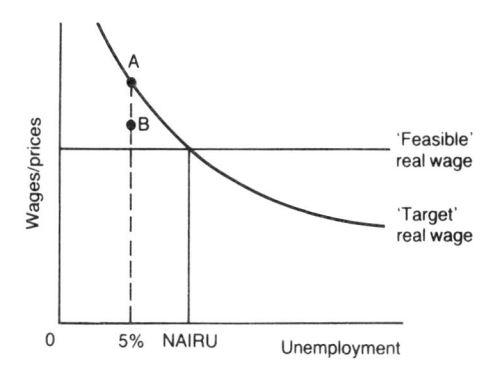

Figure 15 How the NAIRU is determined (see text)

datum. It may also rise somewhat with unemployment, as price mark-ups are reduced. But this does not affect the basic argument.

The statement that the real wage is basically determined by firms may seem surprising, since money wages are determined by wage-bargainers. But in the long run the real wage which the wage-bargainers settle for must be consistent with the feasible real wage. If workers try to set wages too high relative to prices, we shall get upwards-spiralling inflation.

What eventually stops this? The answer is that the wage-bargainers eventually adjust their behaviour. For their behaviour (unlike that of price-setters) depends strongly on unemployment. If inflation is increasing, governments will allow unemployment to increase. This will dampen wage pressure and eventually consistency between the two mark-ups will be restored. Higher unemployment will reduce the target real wage until it is equal to what is feasible.

The restraining influence of unemployment on wage-bargaining is shown in the sloping line of Figure 15. At some level of unemployment there is just enough unemployment to make wage-bargainers settle on the real wage that firms are willing to deliver. That level of unemployment is the NAIRU.

Let us trace out carefully what happens if the government creates so many jobs that unemployment falls below the NAIRU – to, say, 5 per cent. Wage bargainers push up wage inflation above expected price inflation (more, that is, than any difference due to productivity growth). Because they under-estimate the rise of price inflation induced by their actions, they do not hit the real wage at A which they were aiming at, but they do get *some* increase in real wages (as at B). Firms provide this increase because they too under-estimated the rise in wages, and so allowed their price mark-up over actual wages to fall. So rising inflation was the device that reconciled the behaviour of wage-bargainers and the marketing managers of firms. As James Meade has put it, *rising inflation is the only possible outcome if you try to get a quart out of a pint pot.* By the same token, it is only the rising inflation which made it possible for us to have more employment than at the NAIRU.

So we have now gone behind the crude assumptions of Figure 12 to see *why* inflation rises when unemployment is 'too low': it is because low unemployment encourages unrealistic wage behaviour. Equally, if unemployment is very high, the unions get cowed, wages are too low a mark-up on prices, and inflation falls.

Some other concepts

Before analysing the historical experience we need to relate this framework to some of the other terms often used in the discussion of unemployment.

'Keynesian' unemployment

This means the excess of unemployment above the NAIRU – in other words, the unemployment caused by deficient demand rather than the supply-side factors.

All the remaining concepts refer to different forces bearing on the NAIRU.

Seasonal unemployment

Many industries, such as agriculture and construction, operate on a strong seasonal basis, with the result that in slack periods some workers become unemployed. Most of the statistics used by the government are seasonally adjusted, so that this kind of unemployment will not appear.

Frictional unemployment

Even if the economy were to be at 'full employment' there would still be *some* unemployment. This apparent contradiction is explained by the presence of frictional unemployment. Workers leaving jobs often take a little time to find and start new ones, and new workers entering the labour market may stay unemployed for a time while they find out what jobs are available. This type of unemployment therefore represents the operation of the labour market in matching workers with jobs.

Structural unemployment

This aspect of unemployment results from changes in the industrial and occupational structure of the economy. The labour market may only respond slowly to these changes, which implies that in the meantime there are a number of workers who find their particular skills no longer in demand.

Classical unemployment

High unemployment may be associated with 'too high' a real wage. If this is so the unemployment is called 'classical'. Though there have been cases of this type, the more common reason why unemployment is high is that at a given unemployment level workers seek too high a real wage and unemployment has to rise to prevent them getting it.

> **KEY WORDS**
>
> Inflation
> Non-accelerating inflation rate of unemployment (NAIRU)
> Adaptive expectations
> Commodity prices
> Indexation
> Phillips curve
> Real aggregate demand
> Overheating
> Supply side
> 'Feasible' real wage
> 'Target' real wage
> Money wage
> Price mark-up
> Monopoly

Reading list
Friedman, M., Chapter 9 in *Free to Choose*, Pelican Books, 1980.
Layard, R., Chapter 3 in *How to Beat Unemployment*, Oxford University Press, 1986.

Essay topics
1. Governments don't like unemployment. So why don't they spend more until unemployment vanishes?
2. 'To reduce unemployment, we cannot simply stimulate demand. We must at the same time improve our ability to supply the extra output'. Formalize this argument in terms of the model shown in Figure 12.
3. Why is it that the target real wage always equals the feasible real wage in the long run?

Data Response Question 2
Unemployment and inflation

At the annual conference of the Labour party in 1976, James Callaghan, then the Prime Minister, included the following assertion in a speech to the party supporters:

> 'We used to think that you could just spend your way out of a recession and increase employment by cutting taxes and boosting government spending. I tell you, in all candor, that that option no longer exists; and that insofar as it ever did exist, it only worked by injecting bigger doses of inflation into the economy followed by higher levels of unemployment as the next step. That is the history of the past twenty years.'

The causes of unemployment

1. What had been the unemployment situation facing the government over the two or three years previous to this statement (see Figures 1 and 2)? Why were things so bad?
2. What kind of policy is the Prime Minister talking about in the first sentence?
3. Reproduce Figure 12 and indicate a point consistent with a recession. What is happening to inflation at this point?
4. Looking at your answer to question 3, do you agree with the above view that *any* increase in employment will lead to *rising* inflation?
5. Again using Figure 12, indicate which scenario the Prime Minister had in mind.
6. Explain briefly why a fall in unemployment to a very low level is likely to be unsustainable.

Chapter Three
The UK experience

'The biggest single cause of our high unemployment is the failure of our jobs market, the weak link in our economy.' White Paper of March 1985, 'The Challenge for the Nation'

So what is the explanation of our abnormally high level of unemployment? In the very short run, unemployment is determined entirely by the level of spending on British output – that is, it is determined by 'demand'. But over the longer run, as we have intimated in Chapter 2, it is necessary to take into account the 'supply side' of the economy: how much output can the economy supply without increasing inflation? It is this area that will be important in determining where the NAIRU lies. We shall argue that the rise since 1979 has been demand-led.

Up to 1979: supply-side forces
In the years up to 1979 there were a number of changes on the supply side which made it more difficult to maintain full employment without a wage explosion, so that the economy's NAIRU rose over the period. These factors included greater union pressure, wider access to the social security system, and higher taxes on jobs (National Insurance contributions). In addition there was the first oil shock of 1973–74 which made it more difficult to provide workers with the living standards they expected.

These factors tended to raise the 'target' real wage relative to the 'feasible' real wage in the terms of Figure 15, so that the NAIRU increased. For any rate of unemployment below this new higher NAIRU there is a tendency for the rate of inflation to increase. But this rise in inflation cannot continue indefinitely, and eventually the government allows unemployment to rise in order to dampen down wage pressure. Thus in the 1970s unemployment rose as a way of containing wage pressure. As we saw in Figure 13(a), inflation was reduced sharply by higher unemployment – and by incomes policy.

But by 1979 unemployment in the UK had risen only to 4 per cent –

that is about 2½ points above the full-employment level of the 1950s and early 60s. So that was the magnitude by which supply-side forces raised unemployment.

Since 1979: demand-side forces

After 1979 unemployment rose to over 10 per cent – a much bigger increase. This rise was 'demand'-led. It was caused by contractionary **monetary policy** and **fiscal policy**, and by the slowdown in world trade following on the second oil price rise. But Britain was by 1979 a major oil producer and hence uniquely well placed to escape the ill effects of the oil shock. Instead Britain led the collapse, with national output falling by 5 per cent between 1979 and 1981 – more than in any other country.

The motive for contractionary policies was the surge in inflation in 1979–80, which had occurred for three main reasons. First, the incoming government (as in 1974) abandoned incomes policy and gave large public-sector pay rises. Then there was the second oil shock. But, as an oil producer, Britain could have attempted to escape its inflationary effects by using the oil revenues to cut taxes. Instead we did the reverse and increased VAT from 8 to 15 per cent. Inflation shot up, as the non-monetarists had predicted. The government then sent for the fire brigade, in the form not of incomes policy (as in 1975) but of higher unemployment. Let us see what happened.

High exchange rates and tight money

As a result largely of tight money, the pound escalated to a level where it became impossible for whole sections of manufacturing industry to sell their goods at all. Between 1979 and 1983 employment in

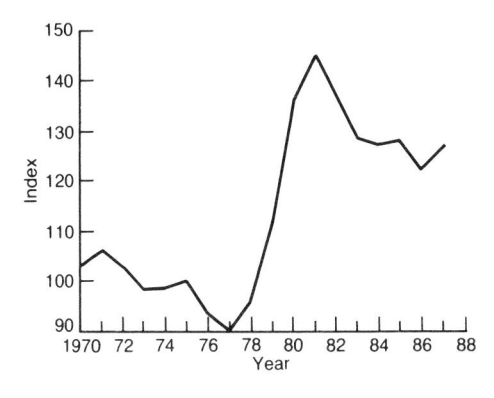

Figure 16 IMF index of relative unit normal labour costs in the UK (1970–79 = 100)

manufacturing fell by 23 per cent. It has shown no sign of ever recovering. In late January 1989 (with the **Sterling Index**, a measure of the pound's value against a weighted basket of 17 other currencies, at 98), the pound was being held at a level where British goods were 24 per cent less competitive in world markets than in the average of the 1970s. Figure 16 shows this loss of competitiveness by looking at an **index of relative unit labour costs** (which compares the UK's labour costs per unit of output with that of a weighted average of its competitors' unit labour costs). The late 1970s and early 80s are associated with a massive increase in costs, which has only ever been incompletely reversed at best.

Tight budgets

There was also a major squeeze on the budget, as shown in Table 5. The share of taxes in national income was raised from 34 to 38 per cent, while government expenditure (as a percentage of potential output) remained virtually unchanged from 1979 to 1981. Similar squeezes happened in other major European countries but the reverse happened in the USA. This provides a perfectly controlled experiment for the effect of budgetary policy. The results can be seen in Figure 17.

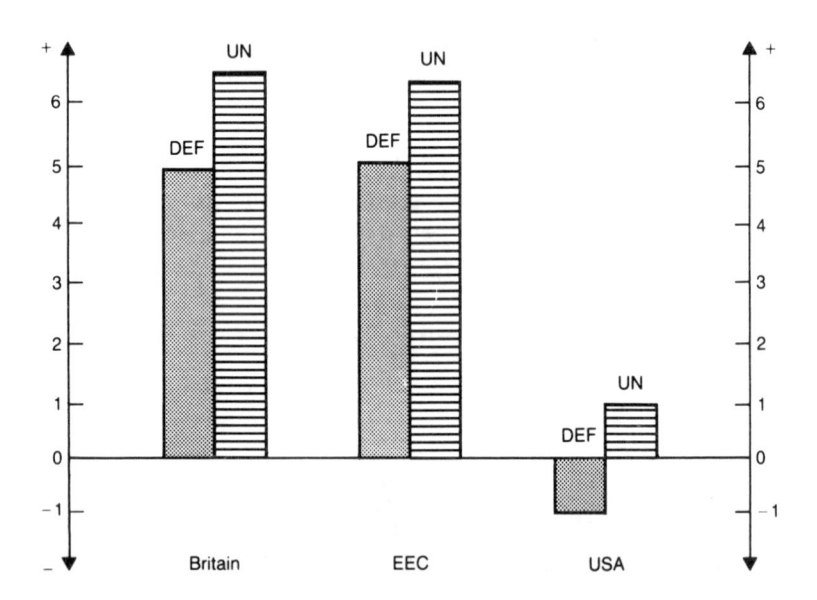

Figure 17 Unemployment and the public deficit (DEF = cut in adjusted budget deficit 1979–86, in percentage points; UN = increase in unemployment 1979–86)

The UK experience

Table 5 Factors affecting aggregate demand, 1970–87

	Taxes as % of GDP at market prices	Government expenditure as % of potential output — Real transfers	Government expenditure as % of potential output — Goods and services	Real short-term interest rate	IMF index of relative unit normal labour costs	Index of real GDP
1970	36.7	11.7	22.9	−0.9	103	80.9
1971	34.8	10.3	22.6	−6.6	106	83.1
1972	33.0	11.6	22.5	−1.9	103	85.0
1973	32.5	12.5	24.0	4.7	98	91.5
1974	35.9	12.3	24.7	−6.0	98	90.6
1975	36.5	11.2	25.4	−16.6	100	90.1
1976	35.8	10.9	24.7	−1.0	94	93.5
1977	34.9	12.5	22.8	−6.0	90	94.5
1978	33.6	13.8	22.0	−0.6	96	97.8
1979	34.3	14.1	22.1	3.1	111	100.0
1980	35.8	14.2	22.4	−5.7	137	97.7
1981	37.9	14.3	21.8	4.6	145	96.6
1982	38.6	15.8	21.5	2.6	137	97.5
1983	38.2	16.1	22.0	3.3	128	101.2
1984	38.3	16.8	21.9	4.5	127	103.3
1985	38.3	18.8	21.3	5.2	128	106.9
1986	38.1	16.9	21.8	7.9	122	110.3
1987	37.5	16.2	21.6	4.3	127	115.2

In Britain and the European Community the budget deficit (appropriately adjusted) was cut between 1979 and 1986 by 4–5 per cent of national income, and unemployment by 1986 was over 5 per cent higher than in 1979. By contrast, in the USA the budget deficit was expanded, and there has been no rise in unemployment compared with 1979. This shows clearly the power of budget cuts to destroy jobs. (It would, of course, have been much better if the USA had achieved this result by a more expansionary monetary policy and a less expansionary fiscal policy. This would have prevented the dangerously high US balance of payments deficit.)

Inflation down but not falling

Thus tight money and budget cuts pushed up unemployment. At the same time they *did* cut inflation. But inflation stopped falling in 1983. Since then underlying inflation remained stable for a long time at 4–5 per cent, and wage inflation at around 7½ per cent. More recently both of these measures have moved significantly upwards. By early 1989 the annual rate of increase in consumer prices had reached 7.5 per cent. Excluding the effects of higher interest rates on mortgage repayments (which are included in consumer prices) the underlying rate was reckoned to be in the range 5-6 per cent. At the same time the annual increase in earnings had risen to 8.8 per cent.

Why has wage inflation been high for so long?

There are three possible factors that could be important here. The first is the huge mass of long-term unemployed people (nearly half the unemployed), who have been out of work for over a year. They have largely given up hope of work, and are often considered as write-offs by employers. Thus an appalling situation has developed in which there is an unemployment culture of people who have given up hope. The Thatcher short sharp shock, which was meant to revitalize the country, has destroyed many peoples' working patterns and, through high unemployment, undermined the work ethic in large areas of the UK. Only recently has the government tried to reverse this situation through the **Restart Programme** of interviews, in which the long-term unemployed are offered advice and encouragement to further their job prospects.

The second factor is that the labour market is split into **insiders**, who are employed, and **outsiders**, who do not have a job but want one. Insiders bargain over wages, but they do so solely in their own interests, without considering the wishes of outsiders. In this case, when a shock leads to large numbers of workers becoming unemployed, they may stay unemployed because insiders will not lower wages in order to increase employment. Consequently wages will not fall when unemployment is high. This factor is probably not as important as the first.

The last factor is the mismatch between the skills demanded in the economy and the skills possessed by the unemployed. As Figure 18 shows, skilled labour is now as scarce as it was in the later 1970s (though less scarce than in earlier times). But for workers without skills (like so many of the unemployed), the market remains almost as weak as ever. The government has now begun to tackle this imbalance through **Employment Training**, but, as we shall see, there is a long way still to go.

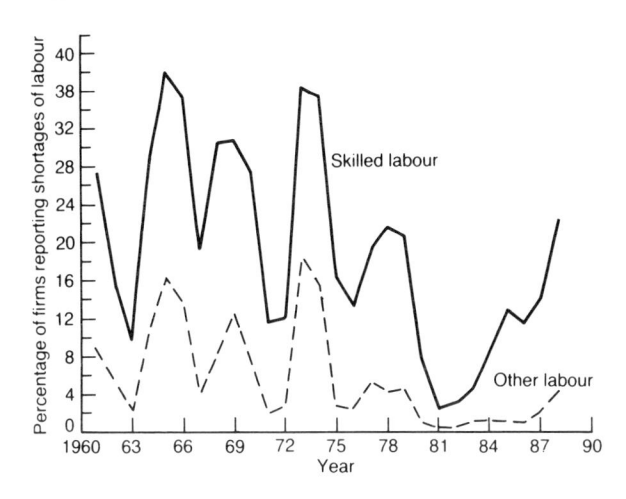

Figure 18 Shortages of skilled and other labour

The Lawson boom

So where are we? During 1986–88 the British economy went through a strong period of expansion. The gross domestic product of the UK rose markedly in this period: by 4.4 per cent in 1987 and an estimated 4.5 per cent in 1988 (see Table 5). This was caused by a surge in investment (starting from a rather low level) and a rise in consumer spending fuelled partly by easier borrowing.

As a consequence of this growth, the workforce in employment (the employed plus self-employed plus HM Forces plus those on work-related government training programmes) has returned to, and exceeded, its 1979 level, as shown in Figure 19. Such a rise may not

UK unemployment

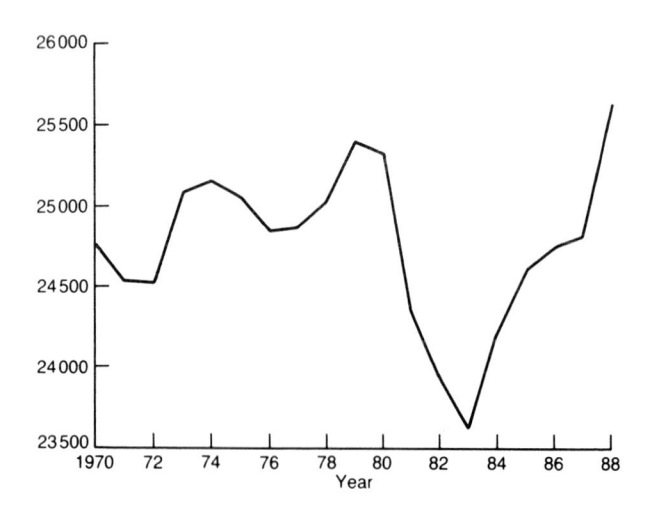

Figure 19 Workforce in employment

imply an all-round rise in *employment* opportunities, however. Firstly this increase includes a rise in the number on work-related government programmes from just 8000 in June 1983 to 376 000 in September 1988. Secondly, although there has been a great improvement in the number of jobs, much comment has been made on the difference between the types of work that have become available and the characteristics of the unemployed who are available to fill them (i.e. on the level of mismatch).

The jobs that have been created have been concentrated in the more prosperous southern regions, in the service industries, and include a large proportion of part-time positions. The rise in these jobs attractive to women can be argued to do little for the 'typical' unemployed worker of Chapter 1, who has a background in industry, is male and comes from the north of the UK. The change in the distribution of jobs is shown in the left-hand side of Figure 20. The greatest increases in employment from 1983 to 1988 came from female full- and part-time employment. Male part-time employment increased by only 169 000 over the five-year period and male full-time employment did even worse, only growing by 139 000.

The growth in employees in employment is only half of the story. A major part of the recent rise in employment has been the growth of self-employment, as shown in the right-hand side of Figure 20. The number of self-employed rose by 766 000 between 1983 and 1988. As the figure shows, this growth seems to have been concentrated

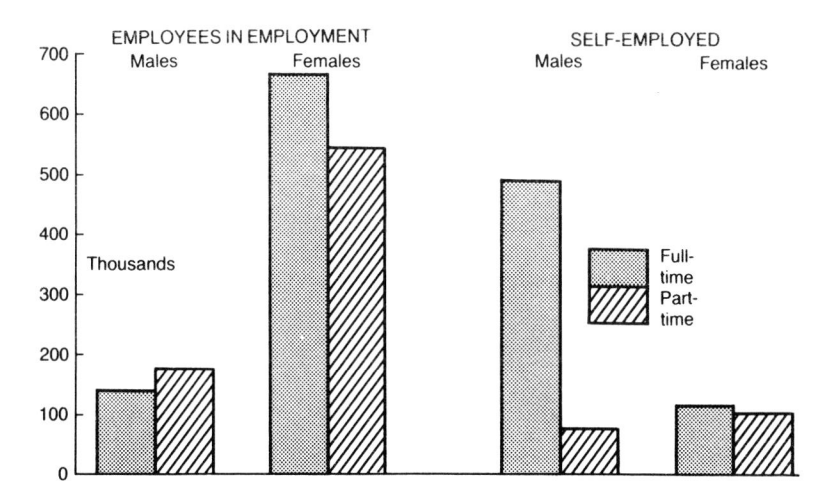

Figure 20 Employment: change from June 1983 to June 1988

amongst males. Whether this is a response to the relatively poor performance of male jobs is a moot point.

This recent growth in employment has led to a large fall in unemployment (see Figures 1 and 2) but to upward pressure on inflation (see Figure 13). The present worry is that the growth in demand has been associated with an upwards drift in inflation and a large current account deficit. The action taken to curb inflation and restore external balance has involved a rise in interest rates in order to dampen domestic demand: see the *Financial Times* article reproduced here as Figure 21. (The O'Shaughnessy piece mentioned in the article is reproduced in the data response question of Chapter 5.)

Don't count on a soft landing

The headline of this article means what it says. It does not rule out a soft economic landing in the UK or anywhere else. It states only that such a landing cannot be guaranteed and it is beyond the power of policymakers to produce it.

Whether the rate of UK inflation can be reduced without a recessionary bump depends on the underlying behaviour of the economy, which is beyond the power of the Treasury or Bank of England to determine by means of their usual tools such as Budgets and interest rates. Nor are there attractive alternative tools remaining unused.

The only guarantee of disaster is if policymakers presume to exercise powers they do not have. Then indeed we can be sure of disruption and thoroughly unnecessary changes.

In the UK there are some signs, for instance in house prices and retail

Capacity utilisation

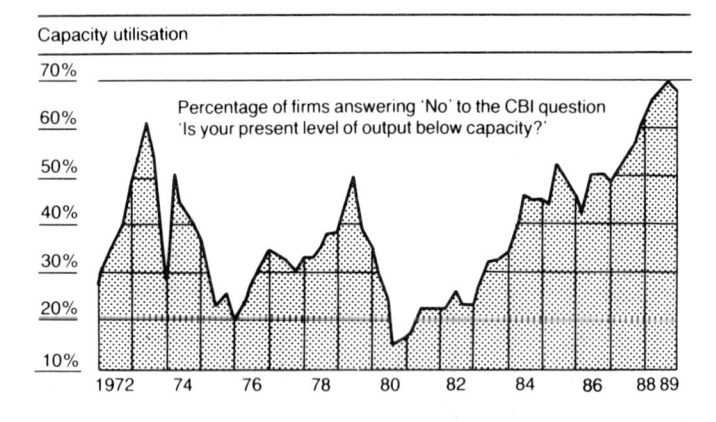

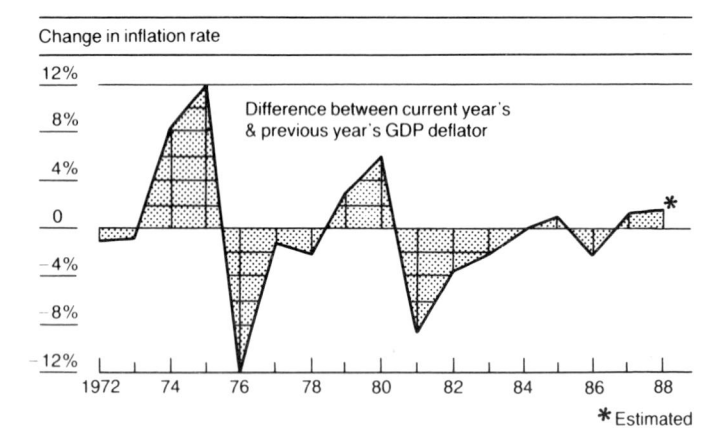

Percentage of firms answering 'No' to the CBI question 'Is your present level of output below capacity?'

Change in inflation rate

Difference between current year's & previous year's GDP deflator

*Estimated

sales, that domestic demand is coming off the boil. But these are still very tentative and could be blown sky high by a fresh set of disappointing indicators for a single month.

Rather more important is the evidence of just how strong the inflationary pressures have been. The rise to 5.3 per cent in output price inflation (formerly called wholesale prices) was indeed paralleled by a similar increase in the cost of materials and fuels – itself due to earlier rises in prices of metals and other basic imports. But the key point is that business managed to pass these increases well and truly on to the customer.

For those with interest and patience, the argument can be taken further. The present rise in inflation can be best understood in the light of earlier debates on the shifting trade-off between inflation and unemployment shown by the so-called Phillips curve. Friedman and other critics argued that only one point or region on this curve was sustainable; and that this was given by underlying real-world characteristics – such as the flexibility of labour markets, geographical mobility, the social security system, training and retraining facilities and much else outside the range of financial policy.

Any attempts by governments and central banks to take a short cut to growth and employment by boosting demand would, they said, lead not just to a one-off rise in inflation, but to an accelerating inflation, which would have to be brought to an end.

These fundamental aspects of the post-Keynesian revolution were for a time overlaid by what Nigel Lawson has rightly called "second order questions" about monetary targets and so forth. But the basic debate has been usefully restarted in the pages of the *Financial Times* in an article on this page on February 1 (Trying to Arrive at a Reasonable Trade-off) by Terry O'Shaughnessy.

O'Shaughnessy's own trade-off is between unemployment and the current balance of payments. As there is some limit to how large and prolonged a deficit overseas investors will finance, we cannot choose our own preferred position on this trade-off either, but have to accept whatever level of unemployment is needed to produce a sustainable balance of payments – pending longer term supply side improvements.

However, I did find a point of contact in Mr O'Shaughnessy's further argument that the main obstacle to full employment might now come from capacity constraints. Indeed, the position of the point of balance known as the NAIRU, or non-accelerating inflation rate of unemployment, has deteriorated so much since the 1960s and early 1970s that it is indeed tempting to switch to some other indicator of excess or deficient demand.

In view of the tendency of excess demand to lead not merely to inflation, but to accelerating inflation, I have put underneath the capacity chart another one showing changes in the annual rate of inflation compared to the previous year. And, indeed, inflation does seem to accelerate when capacity utilisation is high and to decelerate when it is low.

The relationship looks much more dramatic for the 1970s and early 1980s. This was because the average rate of inflation was then in double digits, so that changes in either direction often amounted to many percentage points. There has, however, been no true decoupling, and inflation still rises when utilisation rates increase. Obviously, other forces have also been at work, such as the dramatic oil price increase of 1973-4 and 1979-80, as well as the partial oil price collapse of 1985-86.

Samuel Brittan

Figure 21   From the *Financial Times* of 16 February 1989 (see text)

The outlook for unemployment is therefore uncertain. While the past two years have seen a substantial reduction in this figure, most forecasts predict much slower economic growth in coming years and some indicate that unemployment may stop falling or even rise. This is a terrible prospect while unemployment is still so high.

The basic point is this. Three per cent growth a year will not be good enough. We need something nearer to the 4.5 per cent average growth of 1933–37 and 1987–88 for unemployment to fall substantially. Such growth rates are perfectly possible but they will only happen if, as in the 1930s, the government pursues appropriate

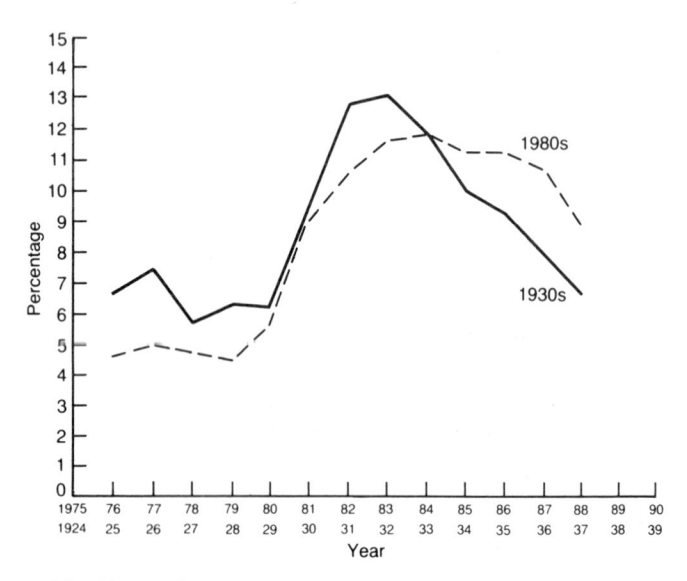

Figure 22 Unemployment rates in the 1930s and 80s

policies. As Figure 22 shows, unemployment has already remained high for rather longer than it did in the 1930s. Unless the government acts now, historians of the future will condemn their economic policies, as they now condemn the policies of the 1930s. The fact is that now, as then, many people can see no alternative to these policies.

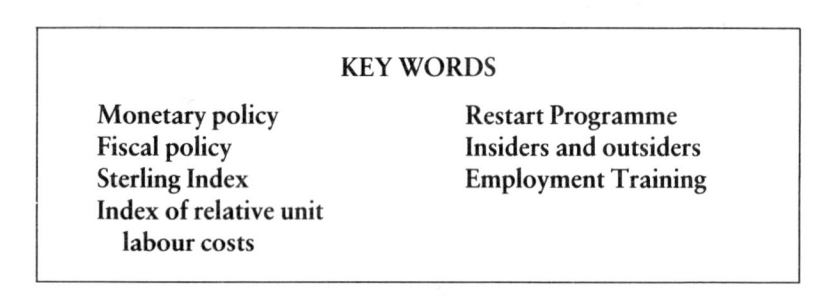

KEY WORDS

Monetary policy
Fiscal policy
Sterling Index
Index of relative unit
 labour costs

Restart Programme
Insiders and outsiders
Employment Training

Reading list

Shields, J., 'Job creation and labour market policy', *Economic Review*, vol. 5, Sept. 1987.

Smith, D., *Mrs Thatcher's Economics*, Heinemann Educational, 1988.

Wickens, M., 'Macroeconomic policy since 1979', *Economic Review*, vol. 5, May 1988.

Essay topics
1. What supply-side factors might affect the NAIRU? Which do you think have been important in recent years?
2. How did demand-side forces contribute to the rise in unemployment in the 1980s?
3. Why might high unemployment not have led to lower wage inflation in the 1980s? Which factors do you think are most important?
4. Considering the UK's experience in recent years, what has been the behaviour of inflation in a time of falling unemployment? How could you explain this in terms of Figure 12? How can the present government's aim of zero inflation be squared with low unemployment?

Data Response Question 3
The three hundred and sixty four

In April 1981 the following letter was sent to the *Times* by 364 British university economists:

'We, who are all present or retired members of the economic staffs of British universities, are convinced that:

(a) there is no basis in economic theory or supporting evidence for the government's belief that by deflating demand they will bring inflation permanently under control and thereby induce an automatic recovery in output and employment;
(b) present policies will deepen the depression, erode the industrial base of our economy and threaten its social and political stability;
(c) there are alternative policies; and
(d) the time has come to reject monetarist policies and consider urgently which alternative offers the best hope of sustained economic recovery.'

This letter generated a large amount of interest. In November 1988 two of the economists wrote the accompanying article in the *Times*. Read the article carefully and answer the questions that follow it.

Were the 364 wrong?

We think it is unlikely that any of those who signed this statement fully appreciated the extent to which it would remain in the public consciousness. Even in 1988 ministers still make speeches referring to the 364 economists. Only a few days ago Sir Douglas Hague, the former chairman of the Economic and Social Research Council, commented that they ought to apologize to Mrs Thatcher.

Against this background, and at a time when the Government's economic policy appears to be confused, we thought that it might be interesting to assess the statement in the light of the government's economic record of the past seven years.

First, with reference to (a), we point out that a 365th economist would have supported our claim that monetary policy on its own could not produce a permanent reduction in inflation combined with a permanent reduction in unemployment. In 1968 Professor Milton Friedman, who provided the intellectual basis for Mrs Thatcher's policies, said that monetary policy could have no long-run effect on the level of employment and output. Indeed, no monetarist has ever been able to offer any convincing theory of why the long-run level of output and employment should depend on the rate of inflation. The output record of high-inflation countries such as France and Italy is not so different from that of low-inflation countries such as Germany and Switzerland.

What do we make of the government's record? There can be no doubt that inflation seems to be under control. But has there been an automatic recovery in output and employment? When we signed our statement there were 2,525,200 registered as unemployed. The number rose to more than 3.4 million in January 1986 and did not fall below the April 1981 total until May of this year. And the definition of unemployment has been changed frequently over the last few years. Any correction for this leads to the conclusion that there are still more unemployed than there were in April 1981. One reason suggested for this is that the long-term unemployed have become unemployable. We hope that the government's new training scheme will do something to rectify this.

The output record is more successful, although not as good as that during the Heath or Macmillan years. Some industrial sectors have been badly damaged. Car output is back to its 1959 level, and during the mid-1980s steel output fell to a level familiar from pre-war days.

We do not say that Mrs Thatcher's policies were solely to blame for this. Many would argue that the trade unions have plenty to answer for. But the facts do not provide evidence that the 364 were wrong. The only part of (b) on which we were incorrect was our prediction of social unrest. Economists should not step outside their area of professional competence.

There is a further issue to consider. We never claimed that recovery in output was impossible; only that the policies of 1981 would not lead to recovery. We observe that between 1981 and 1984 the money supply grew faster than the government planned in 1981. And the public sector borrowing requirement was larger. Any more detailed study would confirm the view that the government did take our advice in (c) and (d), and change its policies.

These changed policies undoubtedly contributed to the expansion which we have seen. But the main reason for the rapid growth in demand and output is that the British public has rejected at least one of the classic Victorian virtues: thrift. Under Mrs Thatcher, consumption has grown much faster than output. Time will no doubt tell whether this is a sustainable pattern of expansion, but an interim judgement has to be that it is a good symptom of living beyond our means.

Very few of those who over the past seven years have attacked our statement have had an opportunity to re-read it. They probably have a blurred image of a bunch of left-wing Keynesians and proceeded to shoot from the hip. As it happens there is almost certainly a consensus of economists throughout the world that (a) is a correct statement. From a scholarly point of view we regret that somewhat dogmatic prediction in (b), not because it was wrong but because a careless reader like Sir Douglas Hague will misinterpret it. We were careful to say "on present policies", and that caveat deserves attention.

We promise that should the balance of payments continue to deteriorate and inflation start up again we shall not claim to have been right. All we shall claim is that we made an honest assessment in 1981 based on such knowledge and understanding which serious economists have. One cannot ask for more.

Frank Hahn and Martin Weale

---

1. How far have subsequent events supported the arguments of the 364 economists' 1981 letter? (Examine carefully the subsequent history of unemployment (Figure 1), output (Table 5) and inflation (Figure 13). Consider the role of the 1985-86 fall in oil prices.)
2. Do you think that the original statement was incorrect?
3. Should the economists apologize?

Chapter Four
Myths about unemployment

'Labour-saving, productivity-boosting technology kills jobs.'
One tabloid newspaper's assessment

The previous chapter outlined our theory of why unemployment in the UK has been so high during the 1980s. Before we move on to consider various proposals for dealing with the problem, we shall analyse some rival explanations.

Myth 1: More technological unemployment

The first myth is widespread. Very many people believe that the rise in unemployment is due to modern technology, and for this reason they are deeply pessimistic about whether we could ever have full employment again. It is certainly true that machines are constantly replacing people, in task after task. But this cannot be why unemployment has increased so much recently. If changes of that kind caused higher unemployment then unemployment would have been rising since the beginning of time. Yet in fact there is no clear trend in unemployment, as Figure 1 showed.

There have been great **productivity** breakthroughs in the past but these have not led to prolonged general unemployment. We had the typewriter, the telephone, the electric motor, the internal combustion engine, the jet engine, and the plastics revolution. Particular workers often lost their jobs. But there was no general tendency to rising unemployment.

When **technical change** actually happens, there are of course changes in employment. Sometimes it goes up (as in the high-tech industries), sometimes it goes down (as with containerization in the docks). Either way there is some dislocation while new patterns of employment are established. But there is no evidence that high productivity growth has normally been a long-lasting source of difficulty. In the UK productivity growth was unusually high in the 1950s and 60s, as in the last six years. But in the 1950s and 60s it caused no unemployment. It was when productivity growth fell in the 1970s that unemployment became a problem – owing to the difficulties of satisfying the demand for higher real wages and living standards. In fact the major country with the lowest unemployment is the one with the highest productivity growth – Japan.

But surely, you might say, high labour productivity (i.e. high output per worker) *must* be bad for employment in the economy. For if output does not rise and output per worker does, fewer workers are needed. But why assume that output does not rise? When it becomes possible to produce more output, the normal result is that more output is produced. This is what has happened over the centuries. The problem today is that output is low in relation to productivity.

The most basic fallacy in economics is the 'lump of output' fallacy: to take output as given. So let us ask instead why the actual output of the economy is lower than it could be. Some people say it is because of satiation – people now have all they need. That view is an insult to all those who live in shabby houses with ill-fed children. There may be some Hampstead trendies or busy stockbrokers for whom extra cash would do no good, but to talk of satiation in general is immoral. The fact is that output is low not because people do not want more, but because they do not have the money to spend. And the government worries about giving it to them, for fear of inflation.

Myth 2: Too many people

Many people think that unemployment is high because of the increase in the **labour force** (from immigration, for example). This is most unlikely. In the nineteenth century the labour force grew much faster than it has recently, with no increase in unemployment. Even in the period 1950-65 the labour force grew as fast as in the 1980s, and we now think of the former period as representing a 'golden age' for low unemployment.

In the short run various factors may influence the labour force and thus may lead to changes in unemployment. For example it could be argued that unemployment in the 1980s was exacerbated by two distinct factors. The first was the **demographic** influence of many more young people coming on the job market as one of the 'baby boom' generations started to turn sixteen. The other was the increased tendency of women to enter the labour force. Between 1981 and 1988 it is estimated that the **activity rate** of women in Great Britain – that is, the percentage of the female population who are either working or unemployed – rose from 47.6 to 50.8 per cent. This activity rate is projected to carry on rising, leading to a larger labour force. This rise, however, will be offset by a 'baby bust' as the number of school-leavers entering the labour market falls in the late 1980s and the early 1990s.

The effects of the labour force on unemployment are short-term: the number of people is not a major factor in the long run. This is confirmed by looking at other countries. As Figure 11 showed, there has been a huge rise in the labour force in both the USA and Japan, but with no great change in unemployment. In the USA, both labour force and employment have risen by about 80 per cent in the last 30 years. The fact is that a normally functioning economy will find jobs for all the people around who want them.

Myth 3: Shortage of capital

So far we have disposed of two myths relating to the *long-term* trend of unemployment: it is not because of more technical change, nor because of too many people. We turn now to a more short-term issue. This is the common notion that unemployment has to be high today because there is not enough capital around to employ the whole labour force.

There can be occasions when this is a problem, as in post-war bomb-shattered Germany. Is it the case in the UK today? The best evidence comes from the answers which the Confederation of British Industries get in their Survey of Industrial Trends. They ask their members in manufacturing industry: 'Is your output over the next four months likely to be limited by shortage of capacity?' The answers are shown in Figure 23. These answers show that for the late 1970s and

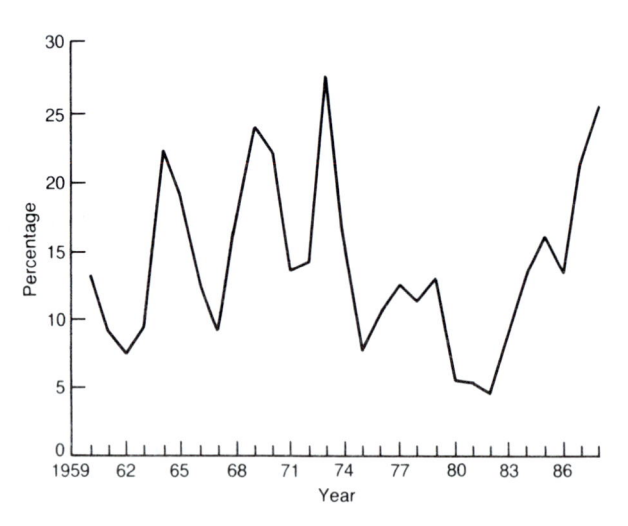

Figure 23 Percentage of firms reporting output to be constrained by shortage of physical capacity, 1960–88

early 1980s there was very little in the way of capacity constraints on firms; but with the rapid growth of the economy over the past few years these constraints have become more important and recently have reached an all-time peak. However, 1988 also saw one of the fastest ever increases in investment. This confirms the view that as capacity becomes scarce, it rapidly adjusts upwards. That is the message that comes from most analyses of investment behaviour, and is supported by evidence from the CBI Survey of Industrial Trends. Firms were asked to indicate whether their reason for capital expenditure was to expand capacity. In the years 1981–83 only 12 per cent of firms indicated that this was so, but as capacity constraints became more important this number rose to over 40 per cent in 1988.

In any case, the notion of capacity is not in any sense absolute. Many different numbers of workers can be usefully employed with a given set of machines. In a given office block or restaurant, the number of workers present can be varied even more. On top of this, extra shifts can be worked. So the quantity of capital is never a continuing constraint limiting employment.

Myth 4: Unemployment would be lower if work was shared out more equally

This is another commonly held view. It states that if everyone were to work *shorter hours*, or *share jobs*, or *retire earlier*, then we could benefit from an immediate reduction in the numbers unemployed.

Let us consider the case for shorter **working hours** per week (the other cases can be analysed similarly). Suppose that the economy is going to produce a certain level of output, so that there are, roughly speaking, a certain total number of hours to be worked each week. If there are people unemployed then it would be better to reduce the hours worked by each worker and increase the number of workers. This would allocate work more fairly and it would reduce unemployment.

This argument seems plausible but there is a critical assumption behind it which is often ignored. It is that output remains constant – or the 'lump of output' proposition. If we reconsider Figure 12, which showed the relationship between unemployment and inflation, then we see that whenever unemployment falls inflation rises more, or falls less, than it would otherwise. So using shorter working hours to cut unemployment leads to a rise in the rate of inflation over what would have occurred otherwise. Two responses are then possible.

Firstly, the government could accept the rising inflation. But if it were to do this then it would obviously have been better to cut unemployment by expanding output rather than redistributing the current amount of work.

Secondly, the government could decide that rising inflation is unacceptable and thus allow unemployment to rise to its former level. The shorter working hours will then have had no final effect on unemployment, but will have decreased output.

There then seems to be little theoretical use for arguing that shorter working hours (or **early retirement** or **job sharing**) present a valid case for reducing unemployment. Let us look at the evidence from different countries, though. Figures 24 shows for each country how unemployment and working hours changed over the period 1975–85 (the figures for Japan, Netherlands, Sweden and the UK are up to 1984, and for France up to 1983). This is worked out on the basis of the average annual hours per person in employment. The diagram shows that shorter working hours seem to be associated with greater rather than smaller rises in unemployment. A very similar picture can be drawn for the increase in early retirement and the increase in unemployment. Both theory and facts then seem to tell against this myth.

General-government net worth* % of GDP

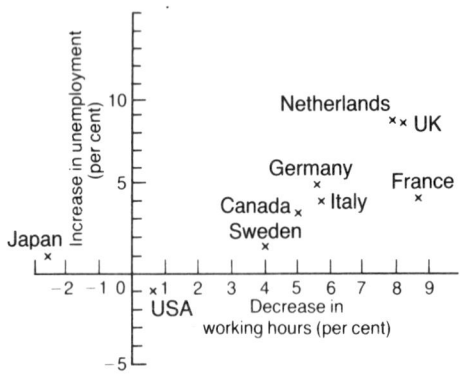

Figure 24 Decrease in working hours and increase in unemployment

KEY WORDS	
Technological unemployment	Activity rate
Productivity	Capital
Technical change	Working hours
Labour force	Early retirement
Demography	Job sharing

Reading list
Heathfield, D., Chapter 22 in *Modern Economics*, Philip Allan, 1987.
Layard, R., Chapter 6 in *How to Beat Unemployment*, Oxford University Press, 1986.
Malinvaud, E., *Mass Unemployment*, Basil Blackwell, 1984.

Essay topics
1. 'High unemployment is not a necessary consequence of modern technology'. Is this true in the short run? What happens in the long run?
2. 'Labour force growth means unemployment growth'. Discuss.
3. Why are capital shortages important? What has been their contribution to the unemployment scene in the 1980s?
4. 'Job sharing is the way to cut unemployment'. Discuss.

Data Response Question 4
Early retirement

Look at the table below, which shows the percentage increase in early retirement and the percentage point increase in unemployment rates for various countries over a ten-year period (1975–85).

	Increase in early retirement (%)	Increase in unemployment (percentage points)
UK	21.4	8.9
USA	14.9	−1.2
Canada	9.2	3.5
Netherlands	19.2	7.8
France	18.8	6.1
Germany	10.6	5.0
Italy	4.2	3.7
Sweden	6.0	1.2
Japan	3.0	0.7

1. Plot the increase in early retirement against the increase in unemployment, in the same manner as shown in Figure 24.
2. Is more early retirement associated with low unemployment?
3. Why might early retirement be thought of as a cure for unemployment? Using the argument of Myth 4 and your answer to question 2, discuss whether this cure will work.

Chapter Five
Remedies for unemployment

'Is it really true that economists can no longer propose policies capable of reducing mass unemployment?' Edmond Malinvaud

What can be done about unemployment? As we argued in Chapter 2, unemployment is determined by supply factors in the medium term and by demand factors in the short term. To reduce high unemployment there must be an increased demand for labour.

But it is no good if this demand simply spills over into higher wages and prices, rather than into jobs. Thus there must be **targeting** of the extra demand towards the slack part of the economy. Viewed in this way the policy also improves the supply capacity of the economy. Two other measures are also important steps in a programme of improving supply performance. The first is an attack on the lack of **training** in the British labour force; and the second is a willingness to tackle inflationary pressures directly through an **incomes policy**. Finally, we need to be sure that in the short run we can avoid an inflationary trade-off due to a speculative attack on the currency. This calls for a suitable **monetary policy**. Let us take these points in turn, beginning with a fuller statement of the problem, and then the four remedies.

The problem
It is not enough for the government to create jobs by spending money itself or by letting private citizens spend more (following tax cuts). It also needs to make sure that the spending does not lead to more inflation. Operating on demand without doing anything about the supply side will soon lead to bottlenecks which will affect inflation. For when unemployment falls, employers will find it more difficult to fill their vacancies. So they will try to attract workers by paying more than the going rate. At the same time unions will feel in a stronger position to push for wage increases, so wage inflation could be a very real problem, leading eventually to higher prices in the shops.

There is also another potential source of inflation. If we try to expand the economy, fears of subsequent inflation could undermine confidence in our currency. This could lead to a fall in the value of the pound, so that we would have to pay more in pounds for anything that we imported. Thus prices in general would tend to rise and the original fears be confirmed.

Our policy should then be to increase demand by only as much as is justified by improvement in the supply side, otherwise lower unemployment will be associated with rising inflation. A strategy for cutting unemployment could achieve this if it takes heed of four basic principles.

Principle 1: Create jobs for the kind of people who are unemployed

It is dangerous to increase spending across the board, so that firms are trying to hire, say, more accountants as well as operatives: accountants are scarce while operatives are not. If vacancies are created for the groups who are already fully employed, then firms will bid up wages, leading to higher inflation.

To avoid this, extra spending must (as far as possible) be targeted towards people who would otherwise be unemployed. This means people who are actually unemployed, or those who are in high-unemployment groups – the young, those in high-unemployment areas, or semi- and unskilled workers.

For long-term unemployed people – a right to work and train

The group most needing help amongst the unemployed are the 40 per cent who have been out of work for over a year. The evidence suggests that such **long-term unemployment** does nothing to restrain inflation, because most long-term unemployed people are so discouraged and stigmatized that they are no longer part of the effective supply of labour as perceived by employers. Most of these people are not near retirement – only 32 per cent are over 50. The majority are in the prime of life, people who would be the backbone of a properly functioning economy. The top priority is therefore to bring the long-term unemployed back to work. To do so would be good economics in terms of both equity and, via the investment in the productive capacity of the country, efficiency.

This requires that such people be given preferential treatment in the allocation of jobs. For example, all employers could be offered a financial inducement for taking long-term unemployed people into regular employment – say £40 per week for the first twelve months of their employment (making £2000 altogether). Such a **job subsidy** would provide employers with an incentive to hire the long-term unemployed instead of other candidates. It is entirely possible that the social benefits to the economy (in terms of equity and efficiency) from the hiring of a long-term unemployed person will outweigh the necessary subsidy.

But justice and efficiency both suggest that we should go further and establish for long-term unemployed people a **right to work or train**. This is the situation in Sweden. There, after 300 days of unemployment, every unemployed person has a right to be offered work or training. The training is high-quality: it costs (per place) 2½ times what is spent on Employment Training in this country, so that ex trainees are well prepared for modern industry, and are snapped up by employers. The jobs are either subsidized jobs in the private sector or public sector jobs on construction projects or in caring activities. By this means unemployment in Sweden has never stayed above 3 per cent and the unemployment culture has never developed. Such a scheme costs money and in 1986 the Swedish exchequer spent 2 per cent of national income on training, employing and placing unemployed adults – compared with ½ per cent in Britain. But in Britain we spent 2.5 per cent of national income on unemployment benefits compared with 1 per cent in Sweden. So the Swedish 'employment principle', as they call it, has justified itself even in terms of purely public accounting, let alone in terms of the social benefits that low unemployment brings.

If Britain had a similar scheme, it would be essential that the jobs available be proper jobs, paid at the going rate. The long-term unemployed want full-time jobs and there is certainly plenty of work that needs doing. There is an estimated backlog of housing maintenance and repairs valued at roughly £30 billion. We also have under-maintained hospitals and schools, and an often sordid environment. And we have lonely and disturbed people, needing home help and community care. In terms of economics, it must promote efficiency if we bring together those needing work with the work that so desperately needs to be done.

According to various estimates it would cost the government between 1.5 and 3.5 billion pounds net to establish such a right to work. This is no more than the net additional resources that currently become available to the government *each year* as a result of buoyant tax revenues. The cost of a right-to-work policy is not too vast and its benefits in terms of human well-being and increased production would be significant. This job guarantee could not only cut the current level of unemployment, it would also be useful in ameliorating the effects of future recessions. As such the scheme presents a viable claim on government resources.

For the high-unemployment regions – a cut in National Insurance contributions

We can also consider special measures to stimulate employment in the high-unemployment regions. Of course money spent on assuring the right to work will automatically find its way to where the unemployed people are. But there is a case for a more general measure. Subsidizing capital is not the right way to proceed if we wish to secure more employment – we need to reduce the cost of labour. One way to cut this cost on a regional basis would be to reduce the employers' **National Insurance contributions** in high-unemployment areas.

For low-paid people – a cut in National Insurance contributions

More than half the unemployed are semi- or unskilled, and this is one reason why they are unemployed. For as a result of modern technology, the relative demand for low-skilled people has fallen sharply (this could be thought of as a case of structural unemployment). Thus, if employers pay a living wage, they will simply not want to employ all the available labour.

There are two possible solutions to this excess of supply over demand. One is to force wages down and supplement pay substantially via Family Credit (and an equivalent for people without children) so that the low-skilled do not suffer. The other is to pay a reasonable gross wage, but ensure that other labour costs for these workers (from employees' NICs) are negligible. Given the economic and political difficulties of bringing down wages for a particular group of workers, the second route is probably preferable. But even that may not solve the whole problem. In this case a wide-ranging scheme of benefits is needed to ensure that, if wages do fall, the living standards of poor people do not.

For reasons of equity one thing cannot be contemplated. We cannot consider denying benefits to people who refuse work which gives them lower net income than they get on benefits, even if the economy would be more productive as a result. Instead we should expand employment that provides a reasonable living standard. This means, first, reducing any extra labour costs to an employer when he employs low-skilled labour; and second, supplementing the income of the worker if the wage is low.

Principle 2: Train everyone

If unemployment arises because of insufficient demand for low-skilled people, one approach is to help direct demand at those with limited skills, as we discussed in Principle 1. The other is to make the low-skilled people high-skilled. This means training not only the unemployed, which we have already discussed, but also (even more importantly) the employed, so that their skills remain up to date and in demand.

There is certainly a great deal of oppportunity for training. By international standards we are a grossly under-trained nation. For example, in Britain 64 per cent of the labour force have no qualifications, compared with 33 per cent in Germany. Whose fault is this? In Germany the training is mostly provided and financed by firms. But experience shows that British firms will not do the job on the proper scale, and half the firms rely on the others to do the training and then poach the trained labour. How can we change the system so that there is an incentive to provide training?

One obvious approach is (within each industry) to tax heavily the firms which train less than the industry average, and use the proceeds to subsidize those who train more than the average. This will provide an incentive for all firms to train more. As it stands the scheme is self-financing and need cost the government nothing, although a certain amount of policing may be necessary. In addition we could, as in Germany, require every employer to provide every employee under 18 with at least 8 hours off-the-job training a week.

This brings us briefly to **education**, which lays the foundation for a trained workforce. The UK's record here is not good either – we have fewer people aged 16–18 in full-time education than almost any other country in Europe. We shall only mention two possible measures to encourage more widespread education. The first is to increase the attractiveness of staying on at school via more sixth-form places, better quality teaching, a wider range of subjects, and so on. The second is to operate a financial inducement by providing a grant to 16-year-olds who stay at school for further education.

So there are plenty of things that could be done, given the money. But there remains the fear that, if we really did expand the economy, even with the maximum of targeting, inflation would still edge up. And the closer the economy came to full employment the worse the inflationary pressure would become.

Principle 3: Incomes policy

Incomes policies are national deals limiting the growth of wages. We have of course had incomes policies before. They have on occasion done good service. In particular, between October 1975 and October 1977 annual wage inflation was brought down from a terrifying 29 per cent to only 8 per cent. This was achieved by incomes policy with no increase in unemployment. By way of contrast, Mrs Thatcher's great reduction in inflation was rather less than that, and achieved at the cost of nearly two million extra people unemployed.

However, the incomes policy of the late 1970s was by no means perfect. It was too rigid to last, for it set an absolute limit to the pay increases for every group. This in effect suspended free collective bargaining, the negotiating process by which employers and unions reach agreement. It was therefore unacceptable to unions, who see collective bargaining as their raison d'être. It was also unacceptable to firms who like to use flexible pay as a method of recruiting, retaining and motivating their workforce. In 1978 and 1979 the policy therefore began to falter.

Any future incomes policy would have to be more flexible in order to avoid these pitfalls. The obvious approach is one based on financial incentives. For example, we can imagine a policy with no absolute limit to pay increases, but which specifies a norm, which applies to the average pay in a firm. The firm can break the norm by awarding large pay rises, but only at a substantial cost to itself. Suppose, for example, the norm were 3 per cent. A firm that raises its average pay by only 3 per cent incurs no penalty. But a firm that raises its pay by 5 per cent would pay a tax equal to, say, the whole of its overpayment. It would thus pay to the Chancellor a tax equal to 2 per cent of its wage bill. This would make firms much more cautious in giving wage increases.

Even if the norm was breached by, say, 2 per cent on average, price inflation would remain constant, given 2 per cent productivity growth and a norm equal to the rate of price inflation. A scheme like this could be easily administered through the Inland Revenue, with a firm assessing its own liability and returning its cheque each time it paid its PAYE.

Before any policy were introduced we imagine that there would be intensive discussion with the TUC and the CBI in order to incorporate the interests of both sides. One would hope then that the norm could be a matter of agreement between the social partners.

There may well be other better alternatives, but there is no way of ignoring the potential inflationary consequences if we intend to substantially reduce unemployment.

The aim is *not* to reduce real wages. It is simply to avoid the pointless increase of *money* wages and prices by the same amount. It would be an awful verdict on any society if it had to maintain a large proportion of its workforce unemployed, just because it could think of no better way of avoiding the wage–price spiral.

Principle 4: Defend the pound, where necessary, by interest rates

The above three principles have described one way, via targeting and an incomes policy, in which unemployment may be reduced without an eruption of domestic wage inflation. The bases are not all covered yet, however. There is always the danger that the **foreign exchange** market will have a sudden panic, forcing down the value of the pound. This would mean that the pound buys fewer dollars. So more pounds would be needed to buy American goods. The result would be higher prices in the shops.

The government has two ways to defend the pound. It can buy pounds in exchange for foreign currency. This reduces our foreign exchange reserves, and its effects cannot always be relied on. A more reliable approach is to raise interest rates. This makes foreigners more willing to lend money to Britain. For this purpose they have to buy pounds. So the flight from the pound is reversed, and its value recovers. Experience has shown over and over again that this method works. Provided we are willing to use it (and known to be willing), there is no reason why the value of the pound should cause us problems. To put the matter another way, since higher interest rates go with less money, we must be willing to contain the growth of our money supply when this is needed to protect the exchange rate.

When President Mitterand tried to reduce unemployment by expanding the French economy in 1982, he did not follow this rule, and he also scared the financial markets with big wage increases and a programme of nationalization. There is no reason to believe that with an appropriate monetary policy, the outcome could not have been more successful.

This does not mean that the present exchange rate is sacrosanct. We are now running a balance of payments deficit on the current account. If we deliberately expanded our economy, the gap between imports and exports would widen further. Does this matter? Should we allow a lower pound, in order to balance the current account?

We should be wary of any uncontrolled depreciation. But when the Sterling Index stands as high as 98 many economists would argue that the pound is over-valued. Some depreciation of sterling would then help to restore competitiveness to UK industry. In order to avoid speculation about the future value of the pound following this fall, sterling could be joined to the exchange rate mechanism of the **European Monetary System**. This move would have the advantage of revitalizing the export sector of the economy, but without triggering a run on sterling which would only add further inflationary pressure to the economy.

KEY WORDS

Targeting
Training
Incomes policy
Monetary policy
Long-term
  unemployment
Job subsidy

Right to work or train
National Insurance
  contributions
Education
Foreign exchange
European Monetary
  System

Reading list

Aldcroft, D., 'Policy response to industrial decline'. *Economic Review*, vol. 5, May 1988.

Aldcroft, D., 'Education and the economy', *Economic Review*, vol. 6, Nov. 1988.

Aldcroft, D., 'Vocational education and training', *Economic Review*, vol. 6, March 1989.

Bazen, S., and Thirlwall, A.P., Chapter 7 in *Deindustrialization*, Heinemann Educational, 1989.

Donaldson, R., Chapters 2 and 14 in *Economics of the Real World*, Penguin, 1987.

Donaldson, R., and Farquhar, J., Chapter 13 in *Understanding the British Economy*, Penguin, 1988.

Levačić, R., Chapters 5 and 6 in *Supply Side Economics*, Heinemann Educational, 1988.

Essay topics

1. Is it practicable to deliver an offer of a one-year job/training to all the long-term unemployed?
2. How could education and training contribute to a fall in unemployment?
3. Could an incomes policy help to reduce unemployment? Could it last? What distortions would it introduce?
4. Can unemployment be reduced substantially without controls over foreign trade and capital movements, and without government involvement in the plans of companies?
5. How can the tax system be used to alleviate unemployment?

Data Response Question 5

Internal and external balance

Read the accompanying article from the *Financial Times* of 1 February 1989, and answer the following questions:

1. Define 'internal' and 'external' balance.
2. What is a 'sustainable recovery'? What would such a recovery require?
3. Define 'current account'.
4. What is a 'shock' in economics?
5. Explain in one paragraph: (a) 'A sustainable recovery would imply movement in a north-westerly direction'. (b) 'The authorities will be forced to consider moving back to the north east'.
6. To what extent is the graph a visual summary of the theme of this book?

Trying to arrive at a reasonable trade-off

Conventional wisdom holds that rapid deterioration of Britain's current account is merely a reflection of a temporary surge in the growth of domestic demand. It does not, therefore, raise serious doubts about the durability of the economic recovery.

I would argue that this is far too optimistic a view. There is no evidence that a sustainable recovery has taken place. On the contrary, unless something changes, the level of unemployment will have to rise again towards – and even past – 3m. The problem is the old one of reconciling internal and external balance. For most of the past 70 years Britain has had to trim domestic economic policy with an eye to maintaining a precarious international and trading position. The evidence suggests that we face the same policy dilemma today.

Consider the figure, which plots the current account balance (as a percentage of GDP) against unemployment for the past 30 years. Two things stand out. First, during short periods, there appears to be a trade-off between external balance – in the shape of a healthy current account – and internal balance, as measured by the level of unemployment. Second, over time, there has been a striking deterioration in the terms of this trade-off.

Thus, between 1958 and 1966 (when the relationship was admittedly a rather weak one) unemployment of about 380,000 was compatible with current account balance. During the late 1960s and early 1970s, the trade-off progressively worsened so that unemployment had to be about 750,000 for external balance.

The oil shock of 1973 exacerbated existing problems. By the beginning of 1974 the level of unemployment consistent with current account balance had jumped to 1,221,000. This new trade off – represented by the middle line on the diagram – held good until the first quarter of 1981 despite the dramatic transformation of Britain from oil importer to oil exporter. It suggests that the rise in unemployment during 1980 and early 1981 was, to some extent, a policy choice and that the *underlying* (zero current balance) rate was still just over one million.

But during the following three years matters deteriorated very badly. Even though the current account stayed in surplus, the cost in terms of unemployment grew. This meant that when domestic demand revived and unemployment began to fall, the current account quickly went into deficit. Between 1981 and 1984 (see the right-hand line in the figure) the level of unemployment consistent with current account balance rose to just under 3m.

There is no evidence that the present recovery is upsetting this pattern. A sustainable recovery would imply movement in a north-westerly direction, off the regression line using 1984–88 data. So far the movement has been south-westerly. It could be argued that a deteriorating external balance is no longer a cause for concern since British residents now own substantial foreign assets and foreigners appear willing to invest in the UK. Evidence for this may be sought in the relative strength of sterling, even in the face of poor current account performance.

The asset position, which resulted from the policy choice to translate oil exports into current account surpluses rather than into an expansion of the domestic economy in the early 1980s, has given room for manoeuvre on the external account. There has certainly also been an important but unquantifiable "Thatcher" confidence effect at work.

The fact remains, however, that the current account will, eventually, assert itself. If the underlying competitive position of the economy does not soon improve – in other words if there is no movement in a north-westerly direction in the figure – the authorities will be forced to consider moving back towards the north-east. The government can certainly reduce the current account deficit by accepting more unemployment, but it is unclear what it can do to improve the terms of this trade-off.

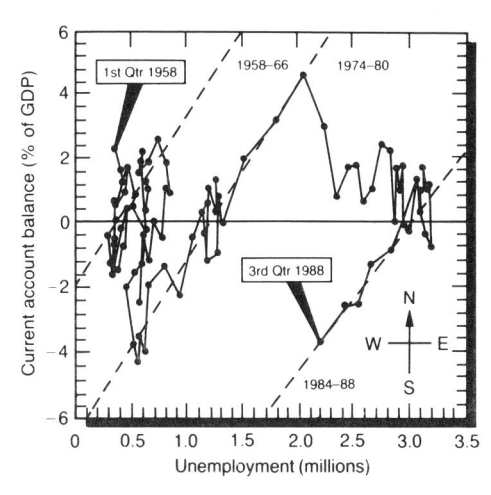

Policy changes which exploit a short-run trade-off between internal and external balance are well understood. But structural shifts in the trade-off itself are more puzzling. What has caused the long-run deterioration in the terms of the trade-off between unemployment and current account balance? In terms of the diagram, why have the regression lines shifted towards the right? There have been two or perhaps three structural shifts of importance: the first in the late 1960s and early 1970s; the second during 1973 and 1974; the third between 1980 and 1984.

Of these the second is easiest to understand since it was an obvious consequence of the oil shock. Comparing the other two, it is clear that what happened in the early 1980s – an increase in the underlying unemployment rate of 1.8m – was several times more serious than the corresponding increase of 370,000 between 1966 and 1972.

But despite the difference in scale, the same mechanism was at work. In both periods the output and capacity of manufacturing industry declined. The collapse was dramatic in the early 1980s, but it is also possible to detect significant deterioration in the mid-1960s and again in the early 1970s.

A deterioration in the terms of the trade-off between current account balance and unemployment has thus occurred at times when investment in manufacturing has been insufficient to provide the production capacity needed in a fully employed economy. Attempts to run the economy without the necessary manufacturing capacity have inevitably led to a deteriorating trade balance in manufactures. While other components of the current account – such as oil – can mask this effect for a period, they cannot provide a long-term respite.

Those who insist on being optimistic can adopt one of two positions. They can dismiss the current account altogether as an indicator of performance or constraint on policy. Adherents of this view are quite happy to sail off in a south westerly direction in the figure – and do not fear the consequences.

Optimists of the second do acknowledge the existence of past and present trade-offs between domestic activity and external balance, but they believe the current recovery will lead to a more competitive economy. Just as the policy choices of the early 1980s led to the accelerated scrapping of equipment and a worsening trade-off between unemployment and current account balance, so the present boom will induce investment in new, efficient plant and shift the whole trade-off back to the left in the future.

In principle, there is something in this. The problem is the scale of new investment required to enable British manufacturing to compete internationally and meet enough of domestic demand to allow the economy to be run at near full employment.

There is little evidence that such investment is forthcoming and none that other sectors can fill the gap. Unfortunately, the likely outcome is that long before domestic investment reaches the necessary levels, the authorities will find it necessary to do more to discourage the boom, thus disappointing optimists of both schools.

Terry O'Shaughnessy

Chapter Six
The objections considered

'No government can guarantee full employment.'   Mrs Margaret Thatcher

We have outlined some ways in which unemployment may be reduced without rekindling inflation. Even so a major programme for training, education and employment would inevitably involve some net cost to the state. Some people would say that we cannot afford it.

Objection 1: Spending on employment and training is self-defeating: it causes inflation and/or raises real interest rates

This is a widespread view and needs to be tackled head-on. Would there be detrimental effects on **wage inflation**, or on the **balance of payments**, or on the public finances, and thus on **real interest rates**?

We can start with wage inflation. The aim of the policies discussed in Chapter 5 is to increase the supply potential of the economy. If the policies increase the effective supply of labour (as they aim to), then an equal increase in the demand for labour can take place without an adverse effect on wages.

The balance-of-payments effects are less straightforward and depend on how the spending programme is financed. If the programme were financed by the government's foregoing planned cuts in income tax, it would actually help the balance of payments; for programmes of training, education, community care and construction all generate far fewer imports than the (first-round) spending induced by tax cuts costing the same amount. And, for the same reason, the number of jobs guaranteed in Britain is much higher. Thus if the programme replaced some policy of equal cost but higher import content, it would actually help the balance of payments.

This would probably be the hard way to finance the programme – at least from the perspective of early 1989; at the time of writing it could be argued that the non-targeted employment rate is as high as can safely be sustained without an incomes policy. And within this total more employment is needed in the traded goods sector, which contributes to our net exports. As we argued at the end of Chapter 5,

63

to stimulate the traded goods sector we need a lower real value of sterling, which may in turn require lower real interest rates. Thus we need a tougher regular budget and a less tough monetary policy. Starting from this position, we can use the public money saved on a tougher budget to finance a supply-side friendly programme of expanded training and job creation.

By considering tight fiscal policy we are not therefore talking in 1989 about deficit finance for employment creation. To foresee the situation in future years is not easy. But the key point is that in Britain public finance is unlikely in the next few years to be an obstacle to job-creation. For our 'national debt' (i.e. **government debt**) is now lower (relative to national income) than in most of the last two centuries. It has fallen sharply since the Second World War, as Figure 25 shows. On present government plans it is set to fall indefinitely. So a moderate budgetary expansion would still permit a falling ratio of debt to income. In these circumstances we could argue that as a result of an employment programme financial markets would not insist on any major rise in long-term real interest rates, which are in any case largely determined at a common world level.

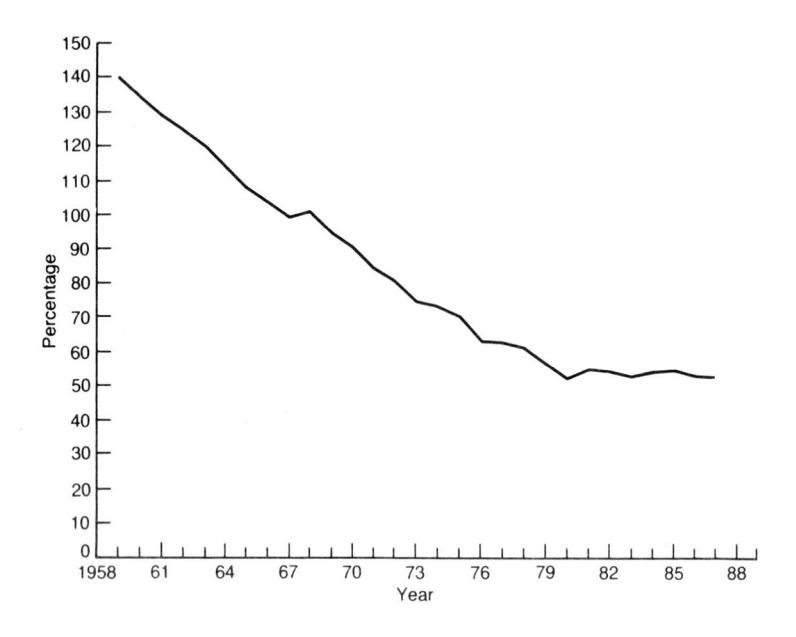

Figure 25 Public sector debt as a percentage of GDP at market prices

There is one point that should be remembered when considering the financial market's response, via interest rates, to the government's debt position: there should be no reason why the government may not borrow money for projects which automatically pay for themselves in money coming back to the Exchequer. This applies to most of what is normally called public investment, as well as to much of education, health and road-building, which increase the country's tax base. Debt corresponding to genuine government investments could in principle be excluded from our calculations of the net debt to arrive at a figure for non-productive debt (say). We could then imagine that it is this non-productive debt which affects interest rates in the market. There is then a case for arguing that, as a productive investment, spending to reduce dole cheques will have less effect on interest rates than if the money were to be spent on other, less productive, causes.

Using this kind of argument it is less likely that a programme of this kind would crowd out other valuable investment projects in the economy. We have also argued that the effect on inflation is designed to be small, and that the balance-of-payments effects could be beneficial.

How do these arguments square up with the government's current plans? In the Chancellor's Autumn Statement (1988) outlays on training and employment were projected to fall by

8 per cent in 89/90
6 per cent in 90/91, and
3 per cent in 91/92.

The explanation given for this is not worries about any of the economic variables cited above, but that unemployment is declining. This brings us to our second objection.

Objection 2: The unemployment problem is no longer serious

This is an insidious argument. It amounts to saying that if a patient's temperature falls from 105° to 104° he is no longer ill. This is what happens if the unemployment problem is judged not by how severe it is but by how it is changing. Of course, if we could guarantee that the changes will continue rapidly in a certain direction for some time to come, then the argument has some validity. However, at present the future movements of the unemployment rate cannot be relied on, so we can argue that the **unemployment level** is more important than the current *rate of change* of unemployment.

To rely on the movement in unemployment as the prime indicator ignores the damage that a high level of unemployment brings in its wake. Unemployment can remain neglected in many quarters because its effects remain unseen. It drives people into their homes. It destroys marriages and impairs health (see the *Guardian* article reproduced here as Figure 26). It stops the will to struggle. Only occasionally does the public see the appalling damage it does. The public notice unemployment when it is increasing rapidly (it might be their own jobs that are on the line) or when the unemployed march to protest against the lack of work. But it is easy to forget.

Yet the fight against unemployment is as much in the interest of the employed as the unemployed. Unemployment benefits and the consequent loss of taxes cost the employed roughly £15 billion, or £600 per worker. Thus unemployment is like an invisible drain in a pond. It lowers the level for everyone. If we tackle unemployment, we shall all gain.

But can it be done? This brings us to our last objection.

Ill-health linked to jobless

The health gap between the unemployed and those in work is widening according to the largest British survey of class health differences published yesterday.

Manual workers and men on the dole are far more likely to suffer angina, respiratory illnesses and raised blood pressure than higher earners.

Their diet is worse, they smoke more, more of them drink to dangerous levels, and they are more fatalistic about their health prospects, the survey involving 22,000 people in Wales shows.

"We hear a lot about the north-south divide, but we now have a rich-poor divide in health terms," said Professor John Catford, director of Heartbeat Wales, the government backed project to prevent heart disease and strokes. "There is no reason why these results cannot be generalised to the rest of the UK."

His findings echo those of the governerment's statistics service, the Office of Population Censuses and Surveys. Its survey of occupational mortality published last summer reveals a health gap growing sharply since 1979.

The Welsh survey shows that people in manual groups are 32 per cent more likely to die of heart attacks and strokes then non-manual workers, and the gap is widening.

Manual groups are two to three times more likely to report symptoms such as angina, breathlessness, and persistent coughs. There is a clear health gradient from social class I to class V. The long-term unemployed suffer most: 41 per cent complain of breathlessness.

Smoking is partly to blame for the different levels of respiratory and cardiovascular symptoms: nearly half the people in social class V smoke compared with under a quarter in class I. The unemployed smoke most of all.

Poor diet is also to blame. Manual groups eat more foods high in saturated fat, such as chips and processed meats, and fewer polyunsaturated

margarines and vegetables. The unemployed in general have the poorest diet.
This is reflected in weight; the lower the social class the more likely people are to be overweight and obese.
More unemployed men drink to excess: 9 per cent drink dangerously compared to 8.5 per cent of men in class V and 4.5 per cent of men in class I.

Andrew Veitch
Medical Correspondent

Figure 26 From the *Guardian* of 19 February 1987 (see text)

Objection 3: Full employment is impossible, so we should adjust to unemployment

According to this view, the main need is to fund creative uses of time for people who do not have paid work. However, our previous argument shows that there are economic gains to be made from putting the unemployed back to work. There are equity gains, as most unemployed people want a paid job in order to avoid feeling disadvantaged, and there are efficiency gains, as national output is lower if we let a valuable resource go to waste.

Society owes its members the chance of paid work. And we *can*, given the will, provide enough jobs. Other countries like Sweden do, and Britain did so for most of the post-war period. If this objection prevails future historians will look back on the 1980s, as on the **1930s**, and marvel at how quickly people assumed that a temporary aberration was permanent.

We could move steadily back towards full employment, if we thought it mattered sufficiently. But do we?

KEY WORDS

Wage inflation
Balance of payments
Real interest rates
Government debt

Unemployment level
Full employment
1930s

Reading list
Stewart, M., Chapter 8 in *Keynes and After*, 2nd edn, Penguin, 1975.
Layard, R., Chapter 11 in *How to Beat Unemployment*, Oxford University Press, 1986.

Essay topics
1. 'We can never return to full employment.' Discuss this assertion.
2. 'The government is not doing more to fight unemployment because it believes that it would be bad for interest rates.' Do you agree?

Data Response Question 6
The national debt

Read the accompanying article from the *Economist* of 25 February 1989 and answer the following questions:

1. For what reasons might public debt be bad for an economy?
2. Are there considerations other than financial ones in evaluating the 'productiveness' of a project?
3. Is public debt used to finance road-building 'good' or 'bad'? Give your reasons. What about debt used (a) to finance training for the unemployed, or (b) to build a park, or (c) to buy bigger company cars for government employees?
4. What is a government's net worth? Why might changes in it not be a good indicator of the attractiveness of a project?

Debt: the zero option

Repaying the national debt is starting to become fashionable. Is this a sensible goal? What level of debt is prudent?

In 1988 the governments of seven OECD economies, including Britain, Australia and Sweden, ran budget surpluses. Several others, including Japan, are closer to budget balance than they were at the start of the 1980s. Indeed in 1989 the average budget deficit of OECD countries as a percentage of their GDPs is expected to be the lowest for 15 years. The ratio of public debt to GDP, which rose sharply in most countries in the first half of the 1980s, is now either falling or broadly stable in every big economy but one – the exception is not America but Italy. On present policies Britain's national debt will disappear around the turn of the century.

Such determination seems impressive. But neither theory nor history offers any guide to the "right" level of a country's national debt. Currently, Italy, Belgium and Ireland all have debt-to-GDP ratios of around 100%, but much higher ratios have been seen in the past: after the second world war Britain's was 200%.

Too much public debt is bad for an economy's health in three ways:

• Investors demand higher interest rates. This may deter private investment and force the currency up, squeezing exports.
• Governments can be tempted to use inflation to erode the real burden of debt.

The objections considered

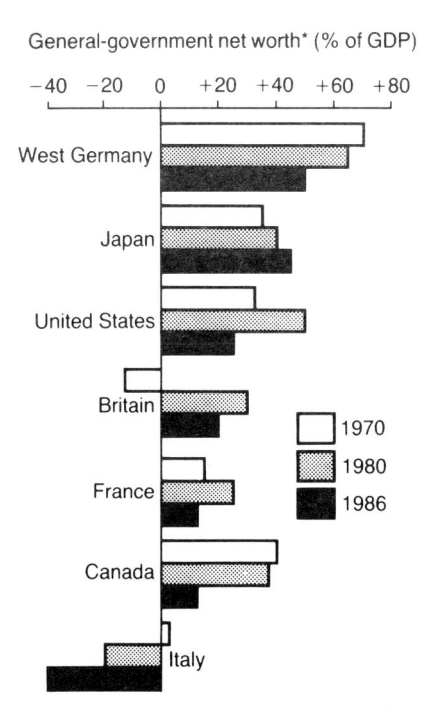

General-government net worth* (% of GDP)

[Bar chart showing West Germany, Japan, United States, Britain, France, Canada, Italy for 1970, 1980, 1986]

Net public debt as % of GDR

	1970	*1980*	*1988*
United States	27.7	19.7	30.0
Japan	−6.5	17.3	24.6
West Germany	−8.2	14.3	23.8
France	11.1†	14.3	26.6
Britain	73.2	47.5	39.1
Italy	34.0	53.6	92.0
Canada	6.1	11.8	36.7

*Fixed capital stock less financial liabilities   †1976.   Source: OECD

● If real interest rates are greater than the growth rate, the debt ratio can rise without limit.

These risks suggest that governments might aim to stabilise the ratio of their debts to GDP. This, however, produces a bizarre result: the higher a government's debt ratio and the higher the inflation rate, the more it can borrow. Back-of-the-envelope calculations show that the Italian government, with a debt ratio approaching 100% and nominal GDP growth of 8%, could happily run a deficit of 8% of GDP and keep its

69

debt ratio constant. West Germany, with a debt ratio of 24% and nominal GDP growth of 5%, would have to run a deficit of only 1%.

Classical economists were almost unanimous in condemning national debt; their advice would be to borrow only in times of war, national emergency or any other crisis, and then repay promptly in peacetime. Clearly, countries like Italy, where public debt is dangerously high, should aim to cut their national debt burden, but not necessarily to abolish it. Not all debt is bad; it can be put to productive uses.

National debt is a government's debt to its own citizens. Unlike foreign debt, which has to be serviced out of export earnings, it is not a real burden on the economy, but a transfer between present and future generations. The right amount of debt will therefore depend partly upon the desired balance between present and future consumption and the desire to smooth out tax rates over time.

Moreover, borrowing to finance productive investment which generates future income or social benefits is surely more prudent then borrowing to pay bureaucrats' salaries. This suggests a better fiscal rule: rather than stabilising their debt, governments should aim to maintain their net worth (i.e. total fixed and financial assets less liabilities). A paper by two economists at the British Treasury, published in 1985, argued in favour of this balance-sheet approach.

The OECD's tentative calculations suggest that governments' net worth (estimated as the replacement value of the fixed capital stock less financial liabilities) has fallen in all the big OECD economies except Japan in the 1980s (see chart). Public investment has been insufficient to maintain the value of the capital stock. In America the government's capital stock fell from 70% of GDP in the mid-1970s to 56% in the mid-1980s; Britain's fell from over 80% to under 70%. These figures should be handled with care because valuing assets at replacement cost overstates their true value. (If a loss-making steel plant were blown up, it would not be rebuilt.) The figures show changes in net worth over time and should not be used to compare levels between countries.

There are many other measurement problems. For example, it can be argued that spending on education and health should be counted as investment rather than as current spending; both add to human capital. And how do you put a value on prisons or public parks which yield little or no financial return but significant social benefits? Despite these qualifications, balance-sheet indicators are still better guides to the appropriate level of government debt than are debt-to-GDP measures.

The balance-sheet approach can also be extended to take account of future unfunded public pension liabilities as populations age. In West Germany, for example, the ratio of old-age pensioners to workers is forecast to rise from 30% now to 41% in 2010, and to 64% in 2030. If the government kept its non-interest budget balance constant at the current level, the OECD estimates that West Germany's net debt ratio would fall from 24% to 5% by the year 2010. Add in the expected rise in pension payments, and the debt ratio jumps to 85% in 2010. The government's policy of cutting borrowing today (and thereby lessening the future rise in taxes) therefore makes a lot of sense.

One caveat: the initial level of net worth cannot be taken as "correct". If bad policies have been pursued in the past, it may be too low. Also, any given net worth can be achieved at many different levels of gross assets – each implying different degrees of government involvement in the economy. The net-worth rule cannot choose between them; at best it indicates whether the government's policies are financially prudent. If the government believes that the resources it claims would be better used in the private sector, then it should invest and borrow less.

Projects

Project A
Attempt to survey what kinds of work need doing in your area and whether the unemployed have the necessary skills. Consider what Employment Training is doing to remedy any mismatch.

Possible sources of information are:

- the local authority's Economic Development Unit
- the Local Employer Network
- the local office of the Training Agency.

Project B
Go to your local benefits office and ask the supervisor or manager if you can survey people in the dole queue, to ask about social and health effects of unemployment as part of your examination studies.

Questions could deal with anxiety, depression, sleeplessness, family relationships, physical illness, financial problems and debt, job search, origin of unemployment, etc.

You should spend some time beforehand preparing suitable questions. Try to avoid 'leading' questions since these would distort your survey.

Index

Activity rate 47
Adaptive expectations 22

Baby boom/bust 47
Balance of payments 36, 63
Booms and slumps 23–24
Bottlenecks 52
Budget deficit 34–36

Capital shortage 48–49
CBI 57
Commodity prices 24
Counting the unemployed 4–7
Crowding out 65
Current account 39, 58

Deindustrialization 13
Demand-side 26, 32–36, 52
Demography 47

Early retirement 49–50
Economic inefficiency 6, 53, 54, 67
Education 56, 63
Employment protection 26
Employment Training 37, 54
Equity 6, 53, 54, 55, 67
European Monetary System 58
Exchange rates 33–34, 52–53, 58, 63–64

Family Credit 55
Feasible real wage 27–28
Fiscal policy 33, 36, 64
Foreign exchange reserves 58
Free collective bargaining 57
Full employment 29, 32, 46, 56, 67

Government debt 64–65
Government expenditure 34–36

Government policy 25, 41–42
Great Depression 1

Hours of work 49–50

Incomes policy 24, 32, 33, 52, 56–57, 63
Index of relative unit labour costs 33–34
Indexation 24
Insiders and outsiders 36–37
Interest rates 36, 39, 58, 63, 64–65
Investment 49, 65

Job sharing 49–50
Job subsidy 53–54

Labour force 18–19, 47–48
Labour Force Survey 2, 14
Labour shortages 37
Lawson Boom 37–42
Long-term unemployment 7–10, 36, 53–54
Lump of output fallacy 47, 49

Manufacturing 13, 15, 33–34
Meade, James 28
Mismatch 17, 26, 37, 38
Monetary policy 33, 36, 52, 64
Money wage 27–28
Monopoly 27

National Insurance Contributions 32, 55
Natural rate of unemployment 24
Nineteen thirties 1, 41–42, 67
Non-Accelerating Inflation Rate of Unemployment 21–29, 32
Non-productive debt 65

73

Official unemployment figures 4
Oil price shocks 2, 16, 24, 26, 32, 33
Overheating 26
Overkill and underkill 25–26

Part-time employment 38–39
Phillips Curve 24–25
Price mark-up 27–28
Productivity growth 25, 26, 28, 46–47, 57

Real aggregate demand 25
Redundancy 10–11
Restart 36
Right to work or train 54

Satiation 47
Self-employment 14, 38–39
Shocks 2, 10, 36
Social Security Act 1988 6
Social security benefits 26
Social security systems 9, 32
Soft landing 39–41
Sterling index 34
Swedish 'employment principle' 54
Supply-side 26, 32–33, 52

Target real wage 27–28
Targeting 52–55
Taxation 26, 32, 34–35, 56, 57, 63
Technical change 46
Trade unions 21, 22, 26, 27–28, 32, 52, 57
Training 52, 55–56, 63, 65

Unemployment
  and health 66–67
  and inflation 21–29, 32–42, 49–50, 53
  benefits 4, 9–10, 12, 54, 66
  by age 11–13, 53
  by industry 13–15, 29
  by region 13–14, 17, 53, 55
  by sex 3–4
  by skill 10–11, 53, 55
  classical 29
  definition of 3–5
  duration 7–10
  frictional 29
  in the USA 2–3
  level and rate of change 65–67
  Keynesian 25, 29
  over time 1–2
  seasonal 29
  structural 17, 29, 55
  technological 46–47
  voluntary and involuntary 10
Unemployment Unit 4, 6
U/V Curve 16

Vacancies 15–17, 21, 52, 53
VAT 33

Wage bargainers 27–28
Wage inflation 8, 52, 53, 56, 63
Workforce in employment 37–38
Work-related government programmes 37–38

Youth Training Scheme 12